THE APOSTOLIC CONSTITUTION
"PREACH THE GOSPEL"
(*PRAEDICATE EVANGELIUM*)

The Apostolic Constitution "Preach the Gospel"
Praedicate Evangelium

With an Appraisal of Francis's Reform
of the Roman Curia
by Massimo Faggioli

LITURGICAL PRESS
Collegeville, Minnesota

www.litpress.org

Cover design by Monica Bokinskie. Cover photo © Vatican Media.

Text of Pope Francis © 2022, Dicastero per la Comunicazione—Libreria Editrice Vaticana. Used with permission.

1	2	3	4	5	6	7	8	9

Library of Congress Control Number: 2022940000
ISBN 978-0-8146-6853-5   ISBN 978-0-8146-6854-2 (e-book)

CONTENTS

Historical-Theological Introduction

The apostolic constitution *Praedicate Evangelium* on the reform of the Roman Curia, promulgated by Pope Francis on March 19, 2022, is one of the most important documents of his pontificate. The work of drafting and finalizing this constitution absorbed the activities of the pope's newly created Council of Cardinals for almost nine years, since September 2013, and it embodies significant aspects of the vision of Francis for the Church. It represents one of the most important efforts to bridge the theology of Vatican II and the institutional dimension of the Church in the Vatican. This reform embodies significant breakthroughs but also visible elements of compromise with the status quo, and, at the same time, it leaves space open for an implementation of the constitution depending on the development of the "synodal process" that will be concluded in October 2023 with the assembly of the Bishops' Synod in Rome. But for Francis, synodality must continue to be part of the new way of being Church. The future of synodality will depend also on the way in which the new Roman Curia as reformed by Francis will interact, in ways that cannot be legislated upon, with the ecclesiology of "walking together" as a people of God.

1. The Roman Curia from Its Origins to the Nineteenth Century

The history of the expansion of the Roman Curia is part of the story of the expansion of papal power in the second millennium, which continues in the third millennium.[1] The central departments for the government of the Catholic Church from its center to its peripheries all over the world, the executive branch of the papacy in Rome acting in name of the pope, which has been crucial for the development of Catholicism in the second millennium (and for the government of the Papal States in central Italy, for centuries until 1870)—these institutions have all grown despite schisms and the Protestant Reformation, secularization, and the loss of temporal power. Just to mention a few examples, the centralized control of theological orthodoxy (the Holy Office), the system of taxation (civil and ecclesiastical), the foreign relations of the papacy, and the procedures governing the appointments of bishops and cardinals all depended for centuries on Rome and the institutions of the Roman Curia.

The origins of the governing body in the Church of Rome around the pope began in the fifth and sixth centuries: the priests (*presbyterium*); the personnel working in administration (*notarii, scriniarii*); diplomats (*apocrisiarii*); the Roman councils (not to be confused with the ecumenical or provincial councils that were the most important decision-making

1. See Niccolò Del Re, *La Curia Romana. Lineamenti storico-giuridici* (Vatican City: Libreria Editrice Vaticana, 1998; 1st ed., Rome: Studium, 1941); *Dictionnaire historique de la papauté* (Paris, 1994); English-language ed. *The Papacy: An Encyclopedia*, gen. ed. Philippe Levillain, English-language ed. John W. O'Malley, trans. Deborah Blaz et al., 3 vols. (New York/London: Routledge, 2002), ad vocem.

body in the Church in the first millennium). In this period there was a distinction between the responsibilities of the pope as a religious leader and his responsibilities as political leader for the city of Rome and in the newly created Papal States, thanks to a forged Roman imperial decree known as *Donatio Constantini* (The Donation of Constantine).

In the first millennium, the pope did not yet work as legislator and judge of the universal Church, and therefore the administrative apparatus was smaller. Things changed at the end of the millennium. From three key roles in the seventh century—the archpriest, the archdeacon, and the head notary—the personnel in the tenth to eleventh centuries grew to seven cardinal bishops, twenty-five cardinal priests, and seven cardinal deacons.

In the eleventh to thirteenth centuries, the administrative offices serving the pope took the official (Latin) name of "Curia." This began a rivalry between the Curia and the ecumenical or general councils of the Church (from Lateran I in 1059 to the Council of Vienne in 1311) that saw in the Curia an obstacle to Church reform. Competition arose between the Curia and the consistories of cardinals as did a dialectic between the papacy and his own appointees, who were facing competition from the Roman nobility and the Roman families that had previously occupied the *Sacrum Palatium Lateranense*. The new institutions of the Roman Curia were the Camera and the Chapel (under Pope Urban II, 1088–1099). The most important element of the Curia after the age of Gregory VII (1073–1085) was the consistory of cardinals, who increased in importance and were drawn from the ranks of theologians and jurists. Under Pope Honorius III (1216–1227), nonresident cardinals were abolished: all of the cardinals had to reside in Rome. This time also saw the invention of the conclave (1059–1274) for the election of the pope, another way to protect the papacy from the Roman aristocracy.[2]

In the thirteenth century the head of the *Camera Apostolica* became the most important member of the Curia. Innocent III (1198–1216) created a new body of judges comprised of pope's chaplains that replaced the cardinals, a specialized judicial body that gradually separated from other papal chaplains who resided in the Roman Curia. To cardinals were reserved questions of jurisdiction and those involving benefices. At the end of the twelfth century there was a centralization in the area of penitence and an increase in the number of sins that could be forgiven only by the pope. The Office of the Penitentiary, the only curial body presided over by a cardinal, was created in the early thirteenth century.

During this period the Curia and the papacy went through the turmoil of conciliarism, the doctrine that advocated a decentralization of the supreme power in the Church from the papacy to the councils of bishops in order to heal the plague of schisms afflicting the Church. The Curia and the papacy survived this challenge and developed their power over the Church, including over the general councils of bishops.[3]

The Curia was made of the papal *familia*—servants and bureaucrats: there was little or no differentiation between private service to the pope and public service. The most important offices were the scribes of the Chancery and the Peni-

---

2. See *Geschichte des Kardinalats im Mittelalter*, ed. Jürgen Dendorfer and Ralf Lützelschwab (Stuttgart: Anton Hiersemann, 2011); Alberto Melloni, *Il conclave. Storia dell'elezione del papa* (Bologna: Il Mulino, 2013).

3. See Francis Oakley, *The Conciliarist Tradition: Constitutionalism in the Catholic Church 1300–1870* (New York: Oxford University Press, 2008).

tentiary. In this period the papacy had a traveling pope, and the city of Rome was not always the administrative capital either of the Papal States or of the Roman Catholic Church. During the Avignon period (1309–1376), the Curia had stability in Avignon with its own buildings.[4]

The consistories of cardinals (weekly meetings) were the most important decision-making bodies in the Church. But there arose the Penitentiary and the Camera Apostolica as the offices that made the whole Curia work; the chamberlain was the closest official to the pope, and the Camera became also a political intermediary under the pope's control. Most of the Curia institutions consisted not of permanent congregations but of "ad hoc" commissions. In 1420 the institution of *datarius* or *datator* was created; this was the future *Dataria*, the body in charge of collecting fees due after an appointment to an ecclesiastical benefice. Until the nineteenth century the Dataria was one of the most powerful institutions of the Curia.

Under Leo X the practice of selling offices extended to the pope's *familia* and the fiscal administration of the city of Rome. The osmosis between the Italian aristocracy and the high spheres of the Roman Curia was typical. The *secretarii domestici* of the pope were the first nucleus of what would become the "cardinal nephew" and later the Secretary of State. Important was the evolution of the Apostolic Camera into a dicastery responsible for managing the temporal revenues of the papacy and, at the same time, the government of the Papal State.

The Council of Trent (1545–1563), like all councils, could not intervene directly in the reform of the Curia; a

4. See Bernard Guillemain, *La Cour pontificale d'Avignon 1309–1376. Étude d'une société* (Paris, 1962).

further reason for this was that the council took place in a city far from Rome. Trent must be seen in the context of a series of failed reforms, not only of the Fifth Lateran Council (1512–1517), at which the Spanish bishops strongly urged (to no avail) the formation of a rotating congregation of bishops in Rome that would safeguard their interests. Pope Leo X and the curia cardinals at his side ensured that this initiative went nowhere. The famous reform plan of 1537, the *Consilium de Emendanda Ecclesia*, also failed, as did the reforms of Pius V between 1569 and 1571. Beginning in 1550, however, a series of reforms of individual congregations (Rota, Penitentiary, Camera) took place, and also noteworthy at this time was the rise of the Holy Office of the Inquisition, which was founded in 1542.

The date of 1588 is the most important in the history of the Roman Curia in the second millennium.[5] Pope Sixtus V's reform fundamentally changed the Curia's previous structure and gave it a shape that it has kept (despite many changes) until today. Sixtus V's bull *Immensa Aeterni Dei* (1588) created the modern Curia in fifteen congregations, each presided over by one cardinal: nine congregations for Church issues and six for temporal matters of state. This meant a reduction of the power of the college of cardinals as such and the beginning of the end for the institution of the "consistory," the meetings of cardinals.[6] *Immensa Aeterni Dei* built on the decision to create in 1542 the Holy Office

5. See Ludwig von Pastor, *Storia dei papi dalla fine del Medio Evo. Sisto V, Urbano VII, Gregorio XIV, e Innocenzo IX (1585–1581)* (Rome: Desclée, 1942), vol. X: 182.

6. See Joseph Lecler, "Le Cardinalat de l'Église romaine. Son évolution dans l'histoire," *Études* 330 (1969): 871–83.

of the Inquisition, which had a supreme role in the Curia, above all other congregations.

This period saw the growth of the power of the Curia in the world Church: more control over orthodoxy and legislation from Rome, and more control over the bishops (visits *ad limina* and papal diplomatic corps, extended by Gregory XIII). In 1586 Gregory XIII set the number of cardinals at seventy. The Curia started to dominate; the pontificate of Clement VIII (1592–1605) was the end of the *concistoro* as a significant body in the Church of Rome.[7]

The seventeenth century opened with the age of the Baroque splendor of Paul V, culminated in the longest pontificate of the century (that of Urban VIII Barberini, 1623–1644), and ended with the program of austerity ordered by Pope Innocent XII. This century saw a great expansion of the curial power thanks to the creation of the Congregation of Propaganda Fide by Gregory XV in 1622: Propaganda would be for centuries the most powerful congregation after the Holy Office because of its authority to govern the churches in mission territories.[8] In this period, there were reforms of the election of the pope, but most importantly the development of bureaucratic procedures that formally established the conditions and qualities required for bishops' appointments (through investigations

7. See Maria Teresa Fattori, *Clemente VIII e il sacro collegio 1592–1605: Meccanismi istituzionali ed accentramento di governo* (Stuttgart: Hiersemann, 2004).

8. See Giovanni Pizzorusso, *Propaganda fide. Vol. 1: La congregazione pontificia e la giurisdizione sulle missioni* (Rome: Edizioni di Storia e Letteratura, 2022); Pizzorusso, *Governare le missioni, conoscere il mondo nel XVII secolo. La Congregazione pontificia de Propaganda Fide* (Viterbo: Settecittà, 2014).

whose reports are collected in Rome) and for the entrance into the prelature by admission of candidates to the level of *referendarius* in the two Signaturas, the first level of the bureaucratic apparatus. A key issue for the Roman Curia in the seventeenth century was the spectacular rise of the role of "cardinal nephew" in the age of nepotism, until its abolition in 1692. The bull against nepotism took an entire decade (1677–1686) to draft and to be accepted by the Roman Curia. The abolition of the cardinal nephew gave space for the creation of the role of Secretary of State, which since the nineteenth century has been the most important political player in the Roman Curia after the pope and together with the Holy Office.[9]

During the eighteenth century the Roman Curia was busy with the need to update its structure for the government of the Papal States (congregations for trade, for maritime commerce, for the economy, and so forth). Pope Benedict XIV (1740–1758), one of the most important legislators in papal history, reformed various congregations of the central administration of the Vatican, but no comprehensive reform of the Curia took place. One way of limiting the influence of the college of cardinals was the creation of "ad hoc" congregations. The congregation that proved to be the most important obstacle to the reform of the Curia was the Dataria (just as it was two centuries earlier, in 1537), as it was connected to the collection of fees and taxes.

---

9. See Renata Ago, *Carriere e clientele nella Roma barocca* (Rome-Bari: Laterza, 1990); Antonio Menniti Ippolito, *Il governo dei papi nell'età moderna. Carriere, gerarchie, organizzazione curiale* (Rome: Viella, 2007); Menniti Ippolito, *Il tramonto della Curia nepotista. Papi, nipoti e burocrazia curiale tra XVI e XVII secolo* (Rome: Viella, 1999).

2. Between the Nineteenth Century and Vatican II

The late eighteenth and early nineteenth centuries, with the French Revolution, the kidnapping of the pope by Napoleon, and the emergency conclave in Venice of 1799–1800, witnessed the nadir of papal power but also the beginning of its resurrection and, with it, of a resilient Roman Curia that had to deal with the most consequential and epoch-making change in its history: the loss of the Papal States in the 1860s, culminating with the invasion of Rome, which became the capital of the new Kingdom of Italy, in 1870.

The century opened with several articulated plans for reform drafted by Curia bishops and given to Pope Pius VII in 1800—to no effect. Some of these plans propose a separation of temporal from spiritual government and a reduction in the number of Curia dicasteries. One of them, in 1814, was censored and withdrawn from public debate.

It was a time of change driven by political events. Even before the Congress of Vienna, in 1814 the new Congregation for Extraordinary Ecclesiastical Affairs was created, which became important in the international political activity of the papacy. The brief restoration of the Papal States after the invasion of Napoleon delayed the plans for a moral reform of the Roman Curia at the service of a spiritual papal power and less for temporal government.[10]

Under Pius IX (1846–1878) the Secretariat of State became the political headquarters of the papacy. The definitive

10. See Lajos Pasztor, "Per la storia della Segreteria di Stato nell'Ottocento. La riforma del 1816," in *Archivum Historiae Pontificiae* (AHP), vol. 5 (1965): 209–72; Pasztor, "La Congregazione degli Affari Ecclesiastici Straordinari tra il 1814 e il 1850," in AHP, vol. 6 (1968): 191–318; Pasztor, "La Segreteria di Stato di Gregorio XVI 1833–1846," in AHP, vol. 15 (1977): 295–332.

loss of the Papal States in 1870 made some important congregations of the Roman Curia superfluous or changed their functions. The Rota, the Signatura, and the Camera Apostolica were no longer also civil tribunals for the Papal States. This also slowly involved the administration of pontifical finances and the Dataria in the reforms of 1897–1898. New offices were created in order to assist the pope in his expanded power to appoint bishops (most importantly, but not only, in Italy).

At the end of the nineteenth century the Curia had twenty-one congregations, three tribunals, and six secretariats—a significant expansion from 1588 but on the same structure created by Pius V three centuries before. In the early twentieth century different plans for Curia reform circulated, but only in 1908 did Pius X (1903–1914) promulgate the major Curia reform made necessary by the loss of the Papal States. With the constitution *Sapienti Consilio,* Pius X reshaped the Curia into eleven congregations, three tribunals, three secretariats, and three offices. A few ancient congregations were eliminated or merged. This reform took stock of the end of the Papal States but at the same time centralized the government of the Church in the Vatican. The offices dealing with international political affairs gained more power (three sections of the Secretariat of State: extraordinary affairs, laws of states and concordats; ordinary affairs in relations with states; preparing and dispatching papal briefs). Pius X assembled a special and secret "small secretariat" around himself to deal with the most sensitive issues, especially the persecution of "modernists."[11]

11. Giorgio Feliciani, "La riforma della Curia romana nella costituzione apostolica 'Sapienti consilio' del 1908 e nel Codice di diritto canonico del 1917," in *Mélanges de l'école française de Rome. Italie et Méditerranée* 116, no. 1 (2004): 173–87.

In 1911 a new regulation for the Holy Office was issued, and in the 1920s many individual congregations, especially for missions, were reorganized. The reform of the Curia was confirmed in the first Code of Canon Law, approved by Benedict XV in 1917. In 1931 there emerged a major—and ignored—proposal for reform of the Curia especially regarding the appointment of bishops and the role of the cardinals and the conclave for the election of the pope.[12]

3. The Issue of the Roman Curia at Vatican II

In the middle of the twentieth century the Roman Curia remained a major problem for the bishops, mainly because of the distance created between the incipient globalization of the Catholic Church and the Vatican's substantially immutable government. The animosity of diocesan bishops against the curial bureaucracy was very visible and pervasive. The Roman Curia had increased its direct influence over the power of the pope and over the bishops in their dioceses.[13]

Until Vatican II there was no real public discussion about the Curia, and under Pius XII the system came to a semi-paralysis in many curial offices, including the Secretariat of State: the normal functioning of the Curia was one of the issues discussed at the conclave that elected John XXIII in October 1958.[14] But the debate on the Roman Curia became part of the more comprehensive plan for an ecumenical (general)

---

12. See *Le gouvernement pontifical sous Pie XI. Pratiques romaines et gestion de l'universel*, ed. Laura Pettinaroli (Rome: École Française de Rome, 2013).

13. On this part, see Massimo Faggioli, "The Roman Curia at and after Vatican II: Legal-Rational or Theological Reform?," *Theological Studies* 76, no. 3 (2015): 550–71.

14. See Andrea Riccardi, *Il potere del papa da Pio XII a Giovanni Paolo II* (Rome-Bari: Laterza, 1993).

council of the Catholic Church, which John XXIII announced on January 25, 1959, to the surprise of (almost) all.

During the ante-preparatory (1959–1960) and preparatory (1960–1962) periods of Vatican II, many bishops requested an internationalization of the personnel of the Curia and spoke against the centralization of Church government. The most pressing issue was the relationship between residential bishops and the congregations and other offices of the Roman Curia.[15] In the proposals sent by the council fathers to Rome for the preparation of the council's agenda, many ordinaries requested more power for the residential bishops vis-à-vis the Roman Curia, the apostolic nuncios, and other Vatican diplomats. This was aiming at a debureaucratization of the work of the bishops, in the sense of freeing them from Roman bureaucracy. Most important was the request for a "stabilization" of the five-year, renewable "faculties" granted by the Consistorial Congregation of the Curia to the bishops and for more power in local liturgical and penitential matters.[16] Few council fathers raised the issue of a more rational Curia system, let alone proposing a comprehensive reform.

During the intersession of 1962–1963 the issue of the Curia remained present in the discussion leading to the draft of the schema on the pastoral ministry of bishops (which led to the decree *Christus Dominus*), which was debated in November 1963. In the previous weeks the great ecclesiological debate of Vatican II on episcopal collegiality had

15. See *Acta et Documenta Concilio Oecumenico Apparando*, vol. I/2, App. 1, *De rationibus inter S. Sedem et Episcopos determinandis* (Vatican City: Typis Polyglottis Vaticanis, 1960), 422–63.

16. See *Acta et Documenta Concilio Oecumenico Apparando*, vol. I/2, App. 1, *De maiore potestate Episcopis concedenda*, 428–63.

taken place. Even more important for the issue of the Curia was Paul VI's speech to the Roman Curia on September 21, 1963. The newly elected pope talked about the reform of the institution, with a promise made to Curia officials that it would be a shared process and not a reprisal against the ecclesiastical bureaucracy that had promoted/expelled (an example of the old adage *promoveatur ut amoveatur*) him to Milan just nine years before.[17] Paul VI planned a reform of the Roman Curia that would not antagonize its members during the unfolding of a still youthful Vatican II.

The proposals for reform made in conciliar speeches never became practical plans, except for the idea of a "central board of bishops" (*consilium episcoporum centrale*) in Rome *above* the Curia.[18] The pope never lost control of the issue, and the idea of such a "central board" was buried on September 15, 1965, when the pope published the motu proprio *Apostolica Sollicitudo* that created the Bishops' Synod. Moreover, the proposal of Cardinal Julius Döpfner of Munich for a reform of the college of cardinals in the shape of a *Senatus Romani Pontificis*—a collegial body to assist the pope that would set aside the historical role played by the Roman Curia—was not considered by Paul VI. The

17. For the text of the speech see *Insegnamenti di Paolo VI*, vol. I, 1963 (Vatican City: Libreria Editrice Vaticana, 1974), 142–51 and *Acta Apostolicae Sedis* 55 (1963): 793–800. For an analysis of the speech, see Alberto Melloni, "The Beginning of the Second Period," in *History of Vatican II*, ed. Giuseppe Alberigo, English version ed. Joseph Komonchak, vol. 3 (Maryknoll, NY: Orbis, 2000), 13–16.

18. About this see Massimo Faggioli, *Il vescovo e il concilio. Modello episcopale e aggiornamento al Vaticano II* (Bologna: Il Mulino, 2005), 389–438, and Antonino Indelicato, *Il Sinodo dei Vescovi. La collegialità sospesa 1965–1985* (Bologna: Il Mulino, 2008), 33–63.

pope chose rather to create a *Synodus Episcoporum*, a purely consultative body and not above the Roman Curia.

But from a theological standpoint the ground had shifted significantly: in the debate of November 1963 and in Paul VI's motu proprio *Pastorale Munus* of November 30, 1963, the new criterion was the need to give back to bishops what Rome had appropriated in the previous centuries. That entailed other changes brought by Vatican II, such as the episcopal conferences and their role in the liturgical reform, which had a deep impact on the perception of the theological legitimacy of the Roman Curia in the eyes of the rest of the Church. One of the most influential theological advisors at Vatican II, French Dominican Yves Congar, noted with his typical verve the meaning of *Pastorale Munus*: "In the end, a list was read this morning of the faculties that the Pope grants to bishops: 'concedimus' [we grant], 'impertimur' [we impart]. Whereas, in reality, all he is doing is to give back—and not graciously—a part of what had been stolen from them over the centuries!!!"[19]

Between 1963 and 1965 the reform of the Curia took the shape of internationalization of its personnel, a wish formulated by Vatican II, received by the pope, and passed on by him to a small group of advisors. A comprehensive reform of the Curia was postponed to the postconciliar times. Part of the institutional reform included a new role for the national bishops' conferences and an age limit for the retirement of bishops. But other key issues, such as procedures for the appointment of bishops and the role of the Vatican

19. Yves Congar, *My Journal of the Council*, trans. Mary John Ronayne and Mary Cecily Boulding (Collegeville, MN: Liturgical Press, 2012), 465. About this, see John W. O'Malley, *What Happened at Vatican II* (Cambridge, MA: Harvard University Press, 2008), esp. 170–71.

diplomatic service, were never debated at Vatican II nor in the post–Vatican II bishops' synods.

4. *The Post–Vatican II Reforms of the Roman Curia*

In the sixty years since Vatican II, the most important reforms preceding Francis's pontificate have been two. The first was issued by Paul VI in 1967. In the fall of 1963, a few months after his election, Paul VI had already appointed a cardinals' commission for the study of the reform of the Roman Curia. This led to the apostolic constitution *Regimini Ecclesiae Universae*.[20] Paul VI's reform inaugurated a new system in the Roman Curia that changed but did not transform the structure created by Sixtus V after the Council of Trent in 1588 and updated by Pius X in 1908. The post–Vatican II Roman Curia was going to become more international, but the career system was not going to change dramatically.

New institutions were created, notably the Pontifical Secretariat for the Promotion of Christian Unity (in 1960), the Secretariat for Non-Christians, the Secretariat for Non-Believers, the Council for the Laity, and the Commission Iustitia et Pax. Other dicasteries changed names.[21] The personnel of the Roman Curia was going to become more international, with a term limit of five years and an automatic cessation of every office at the death of the pope.[22] More

---

20. See Francois-Charles Uginet, "La Constitution 'Regimini Ecclesiae Universae,'" in *Paul VI et la modernité dans l'Église* (Rome: École Française de Rome, 1984), 603–13, esp. 605–6.

21. For a complete list, see Del Re, *La Curia Romana*.

22. See Paul VI, Apostolic Constitution *Regimini Ecclesiae Universae* (August 15, 1967), introduction. The reform of 1967 was completed on

coordination was going to be part of the new Curia, thanks to mixed meetings between different congregations and meetings of all the heads of the dicasteries with the pope. *Regimini Ecclesiae Universae* reset a Roman Curia with four different kinds of bodies: nine congregations,[23] three secretariats,[24] the Council for the Laity, the Commission Iustitia et Pax, three tribunals,[25] and six offices.[26]

But the real change came with the Secretariat of State moving into a very prominent position, with the cardinal Secretary of State in charge also of the new Council for the Public Affairs of the Church and the abolition of medieval and early modern bodies such as the Dataria and the Apostolic Chancery, which were abolished in 1973. The Secretary of State and the Council for the Public Affairs of the Church appear in the first, separate section of *Regimini Ecclesiae Universae* and have the first two places in the Curia, changing an order that had been confirmed by the last important reform by Pius X in 1908.[27] The Secretariat of State was thus in

February 22, 1968, with the publication of the *Regolamento generale della Curia romana* by the Secretariat of State.

23. Congregations for the Doctrine of the Faith, for the Oriental Churches, for the Bishops, for the Discipline of Sacraments, for the Rites, for the Clergy, for Religious and Secular Institutes, for Catholic Education, for the Evangelization of Peoples (Propaganda Fide).

24. Secretariat for Christian Unity, Secretariat for Non-Christians, and Secretariat for Non-Believers.

25. Segnatura, Rota Romana, and Apostolic Penitentiary.

26. Chancery, Apostolic Chamber, Prefecture for the Economic Affairs of the Holy See, Administration of the Patrimony of the Apostolic See, Prefecture of the Apostolic Palace.

27. See Romeo Astorri, "La Segreteria di Stato nelle riforme di Paolo VI e Giovanni Paolo II," in *Mélanges de l'école française de Rome. Italie et Méditerranée* 110, no. 2 (1998): 501–18.

charge of appointments to the Roman Curia. The Secretary of State, unlike the heads of all the other dicasteries, was not appointed for a five-year term but *ad nutum* of the pope. The Secretary of State was to be in charge of papal diplomacy and have the role of coordinating the Roman Curia, like the head of a "super-congregation."[28] The strengthening of the role of the Secretary of the State, making it similar to the rank of prime minister, was a corollary of stronger papal power.[29] Paul VI shaped the Roman Curia vertically, with the Secretariat of State at the summit of the pyramid, in a way that resembled the pope's own leadership in the post–Vatican II period, with Rome directing the institutional reception of Vatican II.[30]

During the decade between 1967 and the end of Paul VI's pontificate, the Roman Curia became more international, especially the Congregation for Religious and the former Congregation of Propaganda Fide, while the pivotal Secretariat of State and Congregation for the Sacraments remained the most Italian of all dicasteries. In 1978, at the end of Paul VI's pontificate, lay Catholics had become (a small) part of every Curia institution, but women still constituted only 8.62 percent of the personnel, and they were all in low-ranking positions.[31]

28. About the Secretariat of State under John Paul II, see Thomas J. Reese, *Inside the Vatican: The Politics and Organization of the Catholic Church* (Cambridge, MA: Harvard University Press, 1998), 175–89.

29. See Riccardi, *Il potere del papa*, 292.

30. See Andrea Riccardi, "L'evoluzione della Segreteria di Stato dopo il 1870," in *Les Secretaires d'Etat du Saint-Siege, XIX–XX siècles*, *Mélanges de l'école française de Rome* 116, no. 1 (2004): 33–44.

31. See Joël-Benoît D'Onorio, "Paul VI et le gouvernement centrale de l'église (1968–1978)," *Publications de l'École Française de Rome* 72 (1984): 615–45.

The reform of Paul VI meant also a growth in the number of Curia personnel: the members of the Roman Curia more than doubled, from 1,322 in 1961 to 3,146 in 1977.[32]

The second important reform was John Paul II's *Pastor Bonus* in 1988. Coming a few years after the new Code of Canon Law (1983), *Pastor Bonus* significantly centralized the Church government in the Vatican and confirmed the superiority of the Secretariat of State and of the Congregation for the Doctrine of the Faith. All this must be seen in the context of the ecclesiological policy of John Paul II and Cardinal Ratzinger, which affirmed the superiority of the "universal" level (Rome) over the local level.[33] The reform of 1988 simplified the structure of the dicasteries, reducing their number (nine congregations, twelve councils, three offices) and creating a system of equals, at least in theory. The structure of the Curia did not change fundamentally, with most changes consisting in the transfer of responsibilities from one dicastery to another. But more powers were given to the Congregation for the Doctrine of the Faith; the bishops' visits *ad limina* every five years became more important for the control of the center over the periphery;[34] and bishops' conferences had a much more limited role than they did during Paul VI's pontificate.[35] Moreover, the ratio-

32. See *The Roman Curia and the Communion of Churches*, ed. Peter Huizing and Knut Walf, special issue of *Concilium* 127, no. 7 (1979).

33. See James Provost, "*Pastor Bonus*: Reflections on the Reorganization of the Roman Curia," *The Jurist* 48 (1988): 499–535.

34. See the *Direttorio per la visita "ad limina,"* published June 29, 1988, by the Congregation for the Bishops and the creation of an *Ufficio di coordinamento delle visite ad limina* within the same dicastery. About this see Provost, "*Pastor Bonus*: Reflections on the Reorganization," 519.

35. See Heribert Schmitz, "Tendenzen nachkonziliarer Gesetzgebung. Sichtung und Wertung," *Archiv für katholisches Kirchenrecht* 146 (1977): 381–419.

nalization and clarification of the dicasteries' tasks stepped back from the reform of 1967.[36] John Paul II's constitution for the reform of the Roman Curia was part of a comprehensive effort that had been codified five years before: *Pastor Bonus* was "an essential part of the new Code of Canon Law of 1983"[37] and, like the Code, was an act of interpretation of Vatican II by John Paul II.

This centralized culture of Church government brought about another step back from Paul VI's reform, which had legislated for the temporary nature of Curia positions: under John Paul II the five-year term limit was seen as an exception more than the rule, especially in certain cases, while Paul VI tended to respect that limit or to renew in some cases for one more five-year term only, thus for a maximum of ten years.[38] Under John Paul II–Benedict XVI, cardinal prefects served on average for longer terms as prefect of the same congregation, for up to sixteen years (for example, Cardinal Grocholewski). A case completely *sui generis* is the twenty-four-year tenure of Cardinal Ratzinger at the Congregation for the Doctrine of the Faith.[39] The frequent celebrations of assemblies of the

---

36. See Provost, "*Pastor Bonus*: Reflections on the Reorganization," 499–535.

37. Carlo Fantappiè, *Storia del diritto canonico e delle istituzioni della Chiesa* (Bologna: Il Mulino, 2011), 308.

38. Only the following were renewed for a second five-year term: Cardinal Secretary of State Casaroli (1969–1979); Cardinal Franjo Šeper at the CDF (1969–1981); Cardinal Agnelo Rossi at Propaganda (1970–1984); Cardinal John Wright at the Congregation for the Clergy (1969–1979); Cardinal Gabriel-Marie Garrone at Congregation for Catholic Education (1968–1980).

39. Cardinal Bernardin Gantin, prefect of the Congregation for the Bishops, 1984–1998; Cardinal Joseph Ratzinger, prefect of the Congregation for the Doctrine of the Faith, 1981–2005; Cardinal Iozef Tomko, prefect of the Congregation for the Evangelization of Peoples, 1985–2001; Cardinal Dario Castrillon Hoyos, pro-prefect and then prefect of the Congregation

Bishops' Synod in Rome (six ordinary synods, the extraordinary synod of 1985, and eight special continental or national assemblies) and the new series of "extraordinary consistories" of cardinals (1979, 1982, 1985, 1991, 1994, and 2001)[40] never really touched the supremacy of a Roman Curia that the pope seemed uninterested in controlling.[41]

Benedict XVI represented an exception. One of the typical features of the "pope theologian" was a lack of interest in the Curia: "Ratzinger continued [John Paul II's] estrangement of the pope from the Curia."[42] In this sense, Joseph Ratzinger was a typical post–Vatican II Catholic academic theologian who saw in the Curia an object lacking theological substance. But Benedict XVI's pontificate did have an impact on the Curia. Some decisions deepened the crisis of Curia that had already been initiated under John Paul II—through a clear recentering on Rome of decision-making processes in the Church. Under Pope Benedict some of the distinc-

---

for the Clergy, 1996–2006; Cardinal Eduardo Martinez Somalo, prefect of the Congregation for Institutes of Consecrated Life and Societies of Apostolic Life, 1992–2004; Cardinal Zenon Grocholewski, prefect of the Congregation for Catholic Education, 1999–2015.

40. About this see Kurt Martens, "Curia Romana semper reformanda. Le développement de la Curie Romaine avec quelques réflexions pour une reforme éventuelle," *Studia Canonica* 41 (2007): 91–116, esp. 107.

41. The apostolic constitution *Universi Dominici Gregis* (On the Vacancy of the Apostolic See and the Election of the Roman Pontiff) of February 22, 1996, confirmed Paul VI's *Romano Pontifici Eligendo* (1975) in the decision that the *vacatio sedis* triggers "a complete deactivation of the Roman Curia" except for the chamberlain, the penitentiary, the vicar for the diocese of Rome, and the vicar for the Vatican: Melloni, *Il Conclave*, 156.

42. Enrico Galavotti, "Sulle riforme della Curia Romana nel novecento," *Cristianesimo nella Storia* 35, no. 3 (2014): 849–90, cit. 887.

tions attempted in previous reforms of the Curia were lost. In February 2006 four Pontifical Councils were merged into two councils, Iustitia et Pax (which absorbed the Pontifical Council for the Pastoral Care of Migrants) and the Pontifical Council for Culture (with the Pontifical Council for Interreligious Dialogue closed but then restored in May 2007). Theologically clear in its intention was Benedict XVI's decision in September 2010 to create the Pontifical Council for the Promotion of the New Evangelization, which remained, however, largely invisible during his pontificate. Even more clear was the new structure given to the Pontifical Commission Ecclesia Dei (created in 1988 for dialogue with the schismatic Society of St. Pius X), which on June 2, 2009, was more closely linked to the Congregation for the Doctrine of the Faith, making the cardinal prefect the president of Ecclesia Dei after the motu proprio *Summorum Pontificum* of July 7, 2007, had expanded its responsibilities for implementing the liberalization of the preconciliar Latin Mass. In other cases, Benedict XVI reordered some responsibilities of the Curia dicasteries: noteworthy was the decision to remove the responsibility for seminaries from the Congregation for Catholic Education and give it to the Congregation for the Clergy.[43] Overall, Benedict XVI did not reform the Curia, nor did he create a commission for the study of the reform of 1988, but his resignation in February 2013 was a powerful signal about the need to reform the Curia.

43. See Lorenzo Lorusso, "Le modifiche di Benedetto XVI alla Costituzione Apostolica *'Pastor Bonus'*: un ponte verso ulteriori riforme," *Iura Orientalia* 10 (2014): 67–83.

5. *The Reform of the Roman Curia from the Beginning of Francis's Pontificate*

Pope Francis has stated in several interviews that he received from the conclave the task to regain control of the Roman Curia after the scandals that became public in 2012 and led, among other things, to the unprecedented trial and the conviction of Benedict XVI's personal steward (the so-called VatiLeaks scandal). Indeed, during the transition from Benedict XVI to Francis the perception of the Curia was significantly different from that in previous conclaves. The fact that very few people expected a new Italian or curial pope from the conclave of 2013 was a symptom of the crisis of the Curia as an institution. The quick election of Jorge Mario Bergoglio, an Argentine who had never been part of the Roman Curia and had had relations with the dicasteries only as a residential bishop, confirmed that expectation.

Francis's reform of the Roman Curia had started well before the publication on March 19, 2022, of *Praedicate Evangelium*.[44] Exactly four weeks after his election, on April 13, 2013, Francis announced the creation of a Council of Cardinals, an advisory panel on Church governance made up of eight cardinals from all continents and with a significant reduction of the Italian and Curia presence.[45] In the chirograph published in September 2013, Francis detailed that the new Council of Cardinals had, among its tasks, to help

44. The *editio typica* was published in *L'Osservatore Romano* on March 30, 2022. The delay from March 19 was due to the need to correct the many typos and add updates needed by the online version.

45. The only Italian was the council's secretary, Bishop Marcello Semeraro, diocesan ordinary of Albano Laziale, until the inclusion in the "C9" of the Secretary of State, Cardinal Pietro Parolin, in July 2014.

him govern the universal Church and prepare a revision of John Paul II's reform of the Curia.

Officially, the beginning of the reform of the Roman Curia under Francis began with a press communiquè of October 3, 2013, on the occasion of the first meeting of the new Council of Cardinals. But already since the beginning of his pontificate, Francis introduced new institutions and new personnel for the economic-financial activities of the Holy See,[46] a stricter control by the pope personally in egregious cases of financial mismanagement by some individual bishops,[47] and a new commission for the prevention of sexual abuse in the Church.[48]

Francis's work on this major project followed three distinct tracks. The first one was the drafting of the apostolic constitution itself: here the Council of Cardinals played a key role, with its forty meetings between 2013 and February 2022 and a very intense phase between 2017 and 2019. In 2017 the title of the new apostolic constitution was announced; in June 2018 Francis received the first draft; most of the five meetings of the Council of Cardinals in 2019 (C9) were dedicated to the constitution, especially in the thirty-first meeting of September 17–19, 2019.

In a long article published in the Italian Catholic magazine *Il Regno* in 2017, Archbishop Semeraro traced the steps Francis had taken so far to reform some aspects of the Curia.

---

46. See the motu proprio *Fidelis dispensator et prudens*, February 24, 2014.

47. Between July and October 2013, the resignations of bishops Anton Stres, Marjan Turnšek, and Franz-Peter Tebartz-van Elst were related to financial mismanagement.

48. The commission was created on March 22, 2014, and expanded on December 17, 2014, with new members.

First, the reform would not create the new position of a *moderator Curiae*, a sort of chief administrator of all the offices, because, according to Semeraro, "the analogy between the Roman Curia and the diocesan curia is not appropriate." Second, the C9 was not just overseeing the reform of the Curia. Semeraro outlined several key principles that were guiding Francis's reform of the Curia. They include the principle of *gradualism of discernment and experimentations* (flexibility); the principle of *tradition as fidelity to history* (no drastic changes); the principle of *innovation* (for example, the new Dicastery for Communication, created between 2015 and 2017); the principle of *simplification* (merging of dicasteries, but also decentralization).[49] It is interesting to note that Francis did not involve the Bishops' Synod or call an assembly of the Synod to discuss the reform of the Roman Curia; further, he involved the college of cardinals only once in the conversation, mentioning the issue in the speech to them for the consistory of February 12, 2015.[50]

The second track was Pope Francis's piecemeal or incremental approach to the reform of the Curia. This took place, first, by adding new dicasteries or changing the structures and competences of the existing ones. On February 24, 2014, the motu proprio *Fidelis Dispensator* instituted the new Council for the Economy and the new "Secretariat for the Economy," of which Australian Cardinal George Pell was appointed prefect. On November 11, 2014, Francis

49. Francesco Semeraro, "Riforma della Curia: in atto," *Il Regno-attualità* 2 (2018): 1–7.

50. See Francis, "Greetings to Cardinals Gathered for the Consistory," February 12, 2015, https://www.vatican.va/content/francesco/en/speeches /2015/february/documents/papa-francesco_20150212_saluto-concistoro -cardinali.html.

established a new judicial body within the Congregation for the Doctrine of the Faith to handle appeals by priests who have been disciplined for sexually abusing children. On September 8, 2015, the two motu proprios *Mitis Iudex Dominus Iesus* and *Mitis et Misericors Iesus* streamlined the process for marriage annulment while also aiming to reduce the workload for Vatican tribunals. In November 2017 Francis added a Third Section to the Secretariat of State that would be in charge of the diplomatic corps of the Holy See. In February 2018 he changed the law to allow non-cardinal bishops serving in the Vatican's bureaucracy to continue to hold their offices past the age of seventy-five, whereas previously they had automatically lost their positions. In July 2018, an Italian lay journalist, Paolo Ruffini, became prefect of the Dicastery for Communication—the first lay man to become prefect of a dicastery of the Roman Curia; in January 2021 a lay man, Professor Vincenzo Buonomo (rector of the Pontifical Lateran University), was appointed leader of the disciplinary commission of the Roman Curia. On February 11, 2022, Francis promulgated a motu proprio entitled *Fidem Servare* that modified the organizational chart of the Congregation for the Doctrine of the Faith by separating the responsibilities into two sections under two different secretaries: the doctrinal section (competent on personal ordinariates; the marriage office to examine the *privilegium fidei* and the dissolution of marriages between two nonbaptized persons or between a baptized person and a nonbaptized person) and the disciplinary section (concerned with crimes reserved to the judgment of the congregation, which are adjudicated by the Supreme Apostolic Tribunal established therein).

A third track comprises Francis's speeches on and to the Roman Curia. The traditional Christmas speeches to the

Roman Curia were particularly pointed and often difficult for the leaders of the dicasteries to hear. In the speech of December 22, 2014, Francis talked about the fifteen diseases of the Curia.[51] That speech was interesting also because Francis tried to frame the Roman Curia in ecclesiological terms, as a "small-scale model of the Church," rather than as a bureaucratic necessity without an ecclesial and spiritual dimension. In the speech of December 21, 2015, Francis presented a list of the twenty-four virtues necessary for the Curia.[52] The speech of December 22, 2016, laid out a twelve-step program for the reform of the Curia.[53] On December 21, 2017, Francis spoke in realistic terms about the task of reforming insti-

51. The disease of thinking we are "immortal," "immune," or downright "indispensable"; the disease of "marthaism" (Martha), of excessive doing (activity); the disease of mental and spiritual "petrification"; the disease of excessive planning and functionalism; the disease of poor coordination; the disease of spiritual Alzheimer's; the disease of rivalry and vainglory; the disease of existential schizophrenia; the disease of gossiping, grumbling, and back-biting; the disease of idolizing superiors; the disease of indifference to others; the disease of a lugubrious face; the disease of hoarding; the disease of closed circles; the disease of worldly profit, of forms of self-exhibition: in https://www.vatican.va/content/francesco/en/speeches/2014/december/documents/papa-francesco_20141222_curia-romana.html.

52. Missionary and pastoral spirit; idoneity and sagacity; spirituality and humanity; example and fidelity; reasonableness and gentleness; innocuousness and determination; charity and truth; openness and maturity; respectfulness and humility; diligence and attentiveness; intrepidness and alertness; accountability and sobriety: in https://www.vatican.va/content/francesco/en/speeches/2015/december/documents/papa-francesco_20151221_curia-romana.html.

53. Individual responsibility (personal conversion); pastoral concern (pastoral conversion); missionary spirit (Christocentrism); organizational clarity; improved functioning; modernization (updating); sobriety; subsidiarity; synodality; Catholicity; professionalism; gradualism (discernment): in

tutions in Rome, quoting the Belgian priest and diplomat de Mérode: "Implementing reforms in Rome is like cleaning the Sphinx of Egypt with a toothbrush."[54] The December 21, 2019, speech connected the forthcoming new structure of the Curia with the ecclesiology of Vatican II and the need to leave medieval Christendom behind.[55]

6. New and Old in Praedicate Evangelium

The apostolic constitution of reform of the Roman Curia was published on March 19, 2022, after exactly nine years from the beginning of Francis's ministry as bishop of Rome. Some delay was due to the COVID-19 pandemic that began in March 2020.[56] The draft was subject to two extensive consultations in 2020. It was revised by the Council of Cardinals and then by the Congregation for the Doctrine of the Faith (CDF) and the Pontifical Council for the Legislative Texts.

Praedicate Evangelium is a very important moment in Pope Francis's pontificate. Compared to expectations during the first few years, it is less a revolution than a traditional

---

https://www.vatican.va/content/francesco/en/speeches/2016/december/documents/papa-francesco_20161222_curia-romana.html.

54. At https://www.vatican.va/content/francesco/en/speeches/2017/december/documents/papa-francesco_20171221_curia-romana.html. Here Francis quoted Archbishop Frédéric-François-Xavier de Mérode, a nineteenth-century Belgian diplomat. Christopher Lamb, the Rome correspondent of *The Tablet* of London, reported that that remark "received no laughter from his audience"; https://www.thetablet.co.uk/news/8294/reforming-vatican-like-cleaning-the-egyptian-sphinx-with-a-toothbrush-says-pope-.

55. At http://www.vatican.va/content/francesco/it/speeches/2019/december/documents/papa-francesco_20191221_curia-romana.html.

56. For example, the April 2020 and June 2020 meetings of the Council of Cardinals had to be canceled.

kind of reform.[57] More importantly, it is consistent with the style of Francis, who has largely governed as a pope without the Roman Curia—and interestingly, it also left the leaders of the Curia not at the center but at the margins of the almost nine-year-long discussion on this constitution.

In the preamble to *Praedicate Evangelium*, Francis mentions the most important dates in the history of the Roman Curia: its foundation in the modern dispensation in 1588 and the reforms that have followed since—by Pius X in 1908, Paul VI in 1967, and John Paul II in 1988. In the post–Vatican II period all popes (except John Paul I for the brevity of his pontificate, and Benedict XVI, who, as the cardinal prefect of the CDF for twenty-four years, had already helped to shape the Curia before being elected pope) felt the need to adjust the Roman Curia to the teaching and the ecclesiology of the council.

It is notable that some of the dreams of the early post–Vatican II period did not materialize: dreams to eliminate the Curia or to divide it into different parts located in different countries, or to move it to Jerusalem, or to effect a radical reduction of its form adequate for a first-millennium ecumenical papacy, before the split with the Eastern Orthodox Churches and the Protestant Reformation.[58] The central

57. See Massimo Faggioli, "For a Reform of the Central Government of a Collegial and Synodal Church Fifty Years after Vatican II," in *For a Missionary Reform of the Church: The Civiltà Cattolica Seminar*, ed. Antonio Spadaro, SJ, and Carlos Maria Galli, foreword by Massimo Faggioli (New York/Mahwah, NJ: Paulist Press, 2017), 358–75.

58. See, for example, Karl Rahner, *Vorfragen zu einem ökumenischen Amtsverständnis* (Freiburg i.B.: Herder, 1974), 29ff.; Joseph Ratzinger, "Prognosen für die Zukunft des Ökumenismus" (1976), in Ratzinger, *Theologische Prinzipienlehre* (Munich: Paulinus Verlag, 1982), 203–14.

government of the Catholic Church that assists the pope is still the Roman Curia, in Rome. The architecture of the new Roman Curia brings changes but not a Francis revolution. True to himself, the Jesuit pope believes more in reforms that do not rely on structural and institutional change but that call for spiritual and cultural conversion.

The first part of *Praedicate* following the preamble, which sets out the theological foundations, is strongly rooted in the documents of Vatican II—especially *Lumen Gentium* (the Dogmatic Constitution on the Church), but also *Christus Dominus* (the Decree on the Pastoral Ministry of Bishops). In Part 2 on the Principles and Criteria, the list is indicative of the core ecclesiological values of this reform: service to the ministry of the pope, co-responsibility, service to the ministry of bishops and to the local churches and bishops' conferences, and the catholicity of the Church. Part 3 on the general norms details the procedures, principles, and structure of the Roman Curia.

The basic structure of the Roman Curia that is spelled out in *Praedicate Evangelium* is still similar to the one created by Sixtus V in 1588. There is a change of names from congregations to dicasteries, but it is still the structure centered on the system of so-called permanent congregations. It is different from the model of the ad hoc congregations that was dominant before 1588 and was replaced by the current system, but it survived in some forms until the nineteenth century. This transition to permanent departments, each led by a cardinal or a bishop, solidified between the end of the nineteenth and beginning of the twentieth century with the disappearance of the system of ad hoc congregations. *Praedicate Evangelium* continues in this trajectory, leading toward a professionalization of the administrative elites but also to a more accelerated turnover of personnel: for Francis, the Curia must *not* be an elite group within the Church. At the same time, this reform also does not expand the space for collegial consultations among cardinals in Rome and with the other cardinals who are residential bishops in the global Catholic Church.

Despite the stated intent to reduce the number of dicasteries, the expansion of the Vatican bureaucracy continues in its trajectory of the last century. We will see the effects on the total number of employees only after the new constitution goes into effect on June 5, 2022, and the permanent departments—which are more numerous than before—are officially set up. *Praedicate Evangelium* lists twenty-eight permanent departments, including dicasteries, tribunals, offices, and units of economic and financial activities. John Paul II's *Pastor Bonus* in 1988 listed twenty-four entities. The increased number does not come as a surprise knowing the growth of the Catholic Church globally.

Compared to *Pastor Bonus*, there are new dicasteries that have been created by Francis during his pontificate. On October 22, 2015, during the assembly of the Bishops' Synod on family and marriage, a new Dicastery for the Laity, Family and Life was announced.[59] In August 2016 Francis announced the creation of a new Dicastery for Promoting Integral Human Development, taking over the competences of the Pontifical Council for Justice and Peace, the Pontifical Council Cor Unum, the Pontifical Council for the Pastoral Care of Migrants and Itinerant People, and the Pontifical Council for Health Care Workers. The Congregation for

59. The statutes were published in June 2016, the apostolic letter *Sedula Mater* of the institution of the dicastery was published on August 17, 2016.

Catholic Education, now merged with the Pontifical Council for Culture, has become the Dicastery for Culture and Education. This will entail, on the one hand (in the section for education), the oversight of thousands of schools and hundreds of universities and, on the other hand (in the section for culture), the creativity necessary to reach out to the world of the arts, sciences, technology, and sports.

Praedicate Evangelium also establishes a new Dicastery for the Service of Charity. Up to this point there has been no parallel to this, as it represents an upgrade of the preexisting office of papal almoner. Something that is not new is the name and function of the financial entities: in this sense, Francis's reform of the Curia is a piecemeal reform that has been done step by step over the past few years. But it is important to note that the Secretariat for the Economy is not among the first-class dicasteries: this is one of the effects of, and responses to, Cardinal George Pell's impetuous and failed attempts to raise the Secretariat for the Economy to the level of the Secretariat of State and of his very public clashes with the Secretariat of State. The Secretariat for the Economy merely "collaborates" with the Secretariat of State, which has "exclusive competence" over matters touching diplomatic functions and anything touching international law. At the same time, the Secretariat for the Economy took charge of managing the personnel of the Roman Curia, taking it away from the Secretariat of State.

Praedicate Evangelium reflects a more global and missionary Church: for example, in the section on the Dicastery for the Laity, Family and Life, article 137 talks about accompaniment, formation, and inclusion not just of divorced and civilly remarried people, but also of those in situations of polygamy, in an echo of the debates at the two assemblies of the Bishops' Synod on family and marriage in 2014 and 2015.

One important feature is that there is now not one dicastery superior to all others but, rather, a stated equality among all dicasteries. Juridical equality among all dicasteries was already stated in *Pastor Bonus*, but it remains to be seen what kind of equality will be the one in the new structure of the Roman Curia. The first, "supreme" congregation in the sixteenth century was the Holy Office, then with Paul VI the Secretariat of State acquired a functional prominence in a kind of competition with the newly renamed Congregation for the Doctrine of the Faith. Now there could be a triad: Dicastery for Evangelization, Doctrine of the Faith, and Secretariat of State.

Indeed, the supreme dicastery is no longer the office in charge of orthodoxy—now the Dicastery for the Doctrine of the Faith. In *Praedicate Evangelium* the first dicastery that is listed is the one for evangelization. With Francis, the primary role once played by the defense of doctrine is now played by evangelization: this is the goal of the reform, a Curia for a more missionary Church. This new dicastery, under the direct control of the pope, combines the Congregation for the Evangelization of Peoples, which governs the Church's administration in missionary territories, with the Pontifical Council for Promoting the New Evangelization, an office launched during the papacy of Benedict XVI. This change comes exactly four hundred years after its predecessor, the Congregation of Propaganda Fide, was founded in 1622 and soon became one of the most powerful offices in the history of the Roman Curia. An institution that disappears completely, after almost a millennium of existence, is the Apostolic Chamber (Camera Apostolica), the papal treasury, for centuries a central body in the papal administrative system.

Bureaucracies are made of laws and paperwork, but also, especially, of people with particular competences, and the

Roman Curia, too, has always been a particular kind of career system. A papal rescript published on November 5, 2014, legislated that Roman Curia bishops retire automatically at the age of seventy-five and that the pope can request bishops to retire even before that age limit. In a document issued motu proprio on February 15, 2018, the pontiff stipulated that bishops serving in the Roman Curia must submit their resignations once they reach the traditional retirement age, but that it will be up to him whether to accept them, so that there is no automatic requirement to retire at that age. *Praedicate Evangelium* builds on those decisions. Article 17 on the turnover of Curia personnel is very important, as it legislates that the term of their appointment is of five years and it can be renewed once. Prefects and secretaries of dicasteries and Curia institutions must submit their resignation to the pope, who will decide, thus leaving the pope some room for exceptions. But there seems to be no exception to the rule that all Curia members lose their office at the age of eighty (the same age limit after which cardinals cannot participate as electors in the conclave to choose the next pope).

Very important is the rule that after five or ten years, clerics and members of religious orders serving in the Roman Curia will return to their dioceses or eparchies or religious orders and institutes. This presents the future of the Curia with the problem of an accelerated turnover, which is not an easy task given that working in a dicastery is a specialized ministry that requires formation but also experience. It will also change a tradition that serving in the Roman Curia is or should be a particular kind of vocation in and for the Church. In this regard, there have been some interesting changes between the last drafts and the final version. Among the differences: the 2019 draft legislated that Curia officials had to have at least four years of pastoral experience before serving in Rome, while the final text says only a more vague *un congruo numero di anni di esperienza* (an appropriate number of years of experience) (art. 14,3); in the 2019 draft the inter-dicasterial meetings were to be coordinated by a new department, while in *Praedicate Evangelium* they are coordinated by the Secretary of State—an evident pushback against this effort to curtail State's authority (art. 34).[60]

The biggest change, and one that has been hailed (sometimes naively) as revolutionary by the mainstream media, concerns the possibility of seeing more lay people in key positions in the Vatican (art. 5). This is potentially revolutionary, but some words of caution are necessary here. One of the biggest novelties of Paul VI's reform of 1967 was the internationalization of the Roman Curia: bringing in more non-Italian personnel in a system dominated by Italians for centuries. It is worth remembering here the proposal made by Spanish cardinal Arcadio Larraona during Vatican II to centralize the needed reform of the Curia and to limit international representation in the Curia to 30 to 35 percent of non-Italians.[61] Internationalization was, in its own way, a request coming from Vatican II and hardly could have been avoided by Paul VI. Sixty years later, we know that internationalization has given us mixed results. There is no going

60. See Dario Menos Torre, "Francisco crea un 'superministerio' para la Evangelización con la nueva constitución apostólica," *Vida Nueva*, April 22, 2019; Lucas Wiegelmann, "Eine Analyse des unveröffentlichten Entwurfs der Kurienreform von Papst Franziskus: Kurie eleison," in *Herder Korrespondenz* 73, no. 11 (November 2019): 33–36.

61. Philippe Chenaux, "La reception du Concile Vatican II dans la Curie romaine," in *The Transformation of the Christian Churches in Western Europe 1945–2000. La transformation des églises chrétiennes en Europe occidentale*, KADOC Studies on Religion, Culture and Society 6, ed. Leo Kenis and Patrick Pasture (Leuven: Leuven University Press, 2010), 255–66.

back to an all-Italian Curia. But curialism and clericalism are not unique to Italians or Italian-born or -educated clergy. And being minimally familiar with Italian (the language but also Italian administrative culture) is still a key asset for working in the Vatican.

Now, one of the biggest novelties of Francis's reform of the Curia is the possibility of having lay people and especially women as members and heads of dicasteries (but not of the Supreme Tribunal of the Segnatura, which is made of cardinals, bishops, and priests).[62] Hiring more women in the Curia has been hindered more by clerical and papal inertia than by theological or canonical obstacles.[63] In this respect, ideological readings of *Praedicate Evangelium* could raise unwarranted

62. On November 4, 2014, Francis appointed Sister Raffaella Petrini as the first female Secretary General of the Vatican's Governatorate, where she served as an official since 2014. On March 24, 2021, Pope Francis appointed Sister Alessandra Smerilli Undersecretary for the Faith and Development Sector of the Dicastery for Promoting Integral Human Development of the Roman Curia; she became, as interim, the first woman secretary of the dicastery on August 26, 2021, and on April 23, 2022, she became the Secretary for the dicastery. On November 7, 2017, Francis appointed two lay women, Professor Gabriella Gambino and Dr. Linda Ghisoni, as undersecretaries of the dicastery. On February 18, 2022, Francis appointed lay theologian Professor Emilce Cuda (together with lay theologian Rodrigo Guerra) Secretary of the Pontifical Commission for America Latina, an institution attached to the Dicastery for the Bishops. On February 6, 2021, Sister Nathalie Becquart, XMCJ, was appointed by Francis as Undersecretary of the General Secretariat of the Bishops' Synod, which is not part of the Roman Curia.

63. On July 13, 2022, Pope Francis appointed three women to the Vatican's Dicastery for Bishops, which assists the pope in the selection of the bishops. The three women (two religious sisters and one consecrated virgin) are personally well known to the pope and within the Roman Curia, and can be seen in some sense as insiders: Sr. Raffaella Petrini, FSE, secretary general of the governorate of the Vatican City State; Sr. Yvonne Reungoat, FMA, former superior general of the Daughters of Mary Help of Christians; Dr. Maria Lia

expectations. It will be interesting to see how the criterion of competence will be applied about lay personnel: competence about what, and compared to whom? For many dicasteries, it is clear that the most competent people from a professional point of view today would be lay men and women, but there is an issue of balance between lay and clerical identity that cannot be solved in technocratic terms of merit. The hiring of lay employees (professors but also administrators) in the pontifical universities in Rome and in Catholic universities in the United States offer an interesting example and a cautionary tale.

Moreover, *Praedicate Evangelium* does not indicate any standards of compensation for experts tapped for Vatican administrative roles. Hiring lay people to work in ecclesiastical administration also means higher costs for personnel compared to those in the clerical state, who receive supplemental income from their dioceses or religious orders. There could be other problems, for instance, if the lay members or leaders of the Roman Curia were to come from new Catholic movements or lay communities that historically have strong ties with Roman clerical circles. They would be able to provide the Curia with lay Catholics that are competent, but they would not be representative of the average Catholic in the global Church. The fact is that the term "lay Catholic" means today vastly different things from what it meant at the time of Vatican II.

A second word of caution: during the press conference in the Holy See press office to present *Praedicate Evangelium*, one of Rome's top canon lawyers, Gianfranco Ghirlanda, SJ,

---

Zervino, president of the World Union of Catholic Women's Organizations and consultant to the Vatican Dicastery for Interreligious Dialogue.

said having lay people and women in key roles in the Roman Curia is possible through a reinterpretation of canon 129 of the Code of Canon Law. This canon allows only priests, those who have been sacramentally ordained to the priesthood, to exercise power of jurisdiction in the Church. But *Praedicate Evangelium* allows such jurisdiction to be exercised after receiving the "canonical mission" from Church authorities and not from sacramental ordination. This could be a positive change, but it also carries risks. Occupying a certain position because of power coming from the sacrament also gives some independence vis-à-vis the institutional Church (there have been centuries of debates about this, including at Vatican II, about the nature of the episcopacy).[64] The perverse result of the new interpretations could be Roman Curia personnel made of lay people but within an ecclesiastical system of allegiance and obedience typical of a more and not less subservient bureaucracy.

Article 76 establishes in the Dicastery for the Doctrine of the Faith a new Supreme Apostolic Tribunal for cardinals, patriarchs, and bishops accused of crimes reserved to the dicastery. Article 78 is one of the most important, as it concerns the Pontifical Commission for the Protection of Minors (PCPM). The PCPM is no longer stuck in the institutional limbo vis-à-vis the Roman Curia that it had been in since 2014 when Francis created it, as it now becomes part of the Dicastery for the Doctrine of the Faith. But the effect of *Praedicate Evangelium* on the efficacy and authority of the PCPM within the Roman Curia remains to be seen.

64. See, for example, Nicolaus Moersdorf, "Munus Regendi et Potestas Iurisdictionis," in *Acta Conventus Internationalis Canonistarum. Romae Diebus 20–25 Mai 1968 Celebrati* (Typis Polyglottis Vaticanis, 1970), 199–211.

We will have to wait and see whether this change helps the commission's authority and independence. Much will depend on the sensibility of the cardinal prefect of the dicastery concerning the issue of abuse in the Church.[65] Article 78 legislates that the PCPM is chaired by a prefect, but it does not specify whether the prefect must be a cardinal (as it has been under Cardinal Sean O'Malley since 2014) or a bishop or whether it can be a lay person. Should the president of the PCPM be a cardinal, there could be a dualism with the cardinal prefect of the Dicastery for the Doctrine of the Faith. If the president of the PCPM is not a cardinal but a bishop or a lay person, that could mean a politically weaker PCPM at the mercy of the leadership of the Dicastery for the Doctrine of the Faith. It will be interesting for historians to go through the different

---

65. In the April 29, 2022, speech during the audience with the members of the PCPM, Francis made clear his intention about the future of the commission: "With the Apostolic Constitution *Praedicate Evangelium*, as the Cardinal mentioned, I formally instituted the Commission as part of the Roman Curia, within the Dicastery for the Doctrine of the Faith (cf. No. 78). Someone might think that this could put at risk your freedom of thought and action, or even take away importance from the issue with which you deal. That is not my intention, nor is it my expectation. And I invite you to be watchful that this does not happen. The Commission for the Protection of Minors is instituted within the dicastery that deals with sexual abuse on the part of members of the clergy. Nonetheless, I have made your leadership and personnel distinct, and you will continue to relate directly with me through your President Delegate. It was placed there, because it was not possible to have a 'satellite commission,' circling around but unattached to the organization chart. It is there, but with its own President, appointed by the Pope. I would like you to propose better methods to enable the Church to protect minors and vulnerable persons and to assist the healing of survivors, in the recognition that justice and prevention are complementary. Indeed, your service provides a proactive and prospective vision of the best practices and procedures that can be implemented in the entire Church."

drafts of this entire section of *Praedicate Evangelium* and see when and why the decision was made to make the PCPM part of the Dicastery for the Doctrine of the Faith.

The new Curia also sends a message about the relations between Francis and neotraditionalist, anti–Vatican II groups: On January 17, 2019, Francis had already abolished the *Ecclesia Dei* commission created by John Paul II in July 1988, whose functions were expanded by Benedict XVI in 2007 with *Summorum Pontificum*. Dealing with traditionalists is now part of the competences of the Dicastery for the Doctrine of the Faith. There is no longer special attention devoted to them with the goal of a possible reunification of the traditionalists with Rome.

A key point is the role of the Secretariat of State. The most visible novelty is that now it has not just two sections but three: the Section for General Affairs (*sezione affari generali*), the Section for Relations with States and International Organizations (*sezione per i rapport con gli stati e le organizzazioni internazionali*), and the Section for the Diplomatic Staff of the Holy See (*sezione per il personale di ruolo diplomatico della Santa Sede*). In a more profound change, Francis has apparently chosen to reduce its role in relation to the absolute prominence Paul VI gave it in 1967. Article 22 of *Praedicate Evangelium* legislates that now the Tribunal of the Segnatura is competent for the conflicts of competence not only among dicasteries as it was in *Pastor Bonus*, but also between the dicasteries and the Secretariat of State. In another difference with *Pastor Bonus*, article 44 specifies that the Secretariat of State is a "papal secretariat": one of the signs that *Praedicate Evangelium* reflects a more pope-centered Curia.

All of the dicasteries are now on the same level, and the Secretariat of State's traditional function as "traffic director" or its role of filter could be weakened. It is not clear whether this will streamline the work of the Curia. Furthermore, according to *Praedicate Evangelium* the Secretary of State need not be a cardinal and not even a priest. But it is hard to imagine a lay Secretary of State because he would have to deal, on behalf of the pope, with bishops and cardinals from a position of hierarchical inferiority. The fact is that there is nothing similar to the figure of the Vatican Secretary of State in the chancelleries of the other Christian churches, particularly in Eastern Orthodoxy. The Secretariat of State represents one of the features that characterize the government of the Catholic Church, the most global and "political" of all churches. When the papacy lost its temporal power in 1870 with the fall of the Papal States, it did *not* give up all its state-like institutions. And one other important question obviously not addressed by the apostolic constitution is how Italian the Secretariat of State will continue to be. As unpopular as this may sound, being Italian has helped Secretaries of State navigate the rough waters of intra-Vatican, ecclesiastical, and secular politics. But it has also made them more liable to a cardinal-nephew–like interpretation of their role (see Cardinal Tarcisio Bertone, 2006–2013). Recent experiences of non-Italians at the helm of the Secretariat of State made more sense with an Italian pope (see Cardinal Jean-Marie Villot, 1969–1979). But it is much more likely that there will be more non-Italian cardinal Secretaries of State instead of lay ones.

It must be noted that *Praedicate Evangelium* never mentions the Council of Cardinals, a body Francis created in April 2013, exactly four weeks after his election. The decision not to include this "privy council" in the new apostolic constitution might reassure the Vatican's old guard that the pope has implemented a reform, not a revolution. Creating a permanent role for a Council of Cardinals helping the pope govern the Church and the Curia would have been a more revolutionary change, but also it would have been a way to be faithful to one of the requests advanced during Vatican II.[66] It remains to be seen what will happen to the Council of Cardinals after the end of Francis's pontificate. Francis has given his successor(s) total freedom to decide whether or not to continue having the Council of Cardinals.

The relationship among the pope, the cardinals, and the Curia has been very complex historically. Vatican II added one more institution that is not part of the Roman Curia but whose general secretariat is in the Vatican: the Bishops' Synod. Now, both the Roman Curia and the Bishops' Synod are extensions of papal primacy. It is still not clear how the implementation of *Praedicate Evangelium* might change the relationship between the Curia and the Bishops' Synod, which the apostolic constitution now simply calls "the Synod." The same article 33 mentions the need for cooperation between the Roman Curia and the General Secretariat of the Synod: both must cooperate with the pope, but there are no specifications about the relations between the two—and this must be seen in the context of the "synodal process" 2021–2023 leading to the Synod of Bishops' assembly of October 2023.

Similarly, there is only a very short passage (art. 35, not very different from *Pastor Bonus*) on the consistories—meetings of all cardinals called by the pope to discuss particularly important issues. Francis convened an extraordinary consistory of all the world's cardinals only once, on February 20–21, 2014, on the theme of the family. There is also a similar

66. On this see Faggioli, *Il vescovo e il concilio.*

question mark over the relationship between meetings of all Curia prefects and the frequency of those meetings, which now, according to article 34, are called and coordinated by the Secretary of State in agreement with the pope.

A key congregation of the Curia has always been the one for the bishops. The new Dicastery for the Bishops lost its competency over the personal prelatures (Opus Dei), which are now under the Dicastery for the Clergy. More importantly, it will be interesting to see how the new Curia responds to demands for a more synodal way of preparing diocesan bishops' once-every-five-years *ad limina* visits to Rome and bishops' appointments. The Australians, for instance, in the context of the Plenary Council that is being celebrated in their country, have urged a new way of preparing these visits.[67] Articles 38–42 on the *ad limina* visits are not fundamentally different from the ones in John Paul II's *Pastor Bonus*. It remains to be seen how the application of *Praedicate Evangelium* will receive those proposals. Article 105 on the bishops' appointments has an interesting addition compared to the text of *Pastor Bonus*, as it specifies the possibility of involving, "in ways that are appropriate," in this process the people of God in the dioceses that need a new bishop.

---

67. For example, in light of the complicated experience of the visit *ad limina* of 1998. See, for example, the proposals coming from "The Light from the Southern Cross," a 200–page document on ecclesial governance written between 2019 and 2020 by a task force set up by the Australian Catholic Bishops' Conference (ACBC) and the conference of men and women religious of Australia (CRA) and tasked with formulating proposals for Church reform in light of the abuse crisis. See Richard Lennan, "The Ecclesiology of The Light from the Southern Cross," in *Australasian Catholic Record* 98, no. 3 (2021): 284–97. (Full disclosure: I was, together with Richard Lennan, one of the four external experts called to work with the task force.)

7. The Implementation of Praedicate Evangelium

On May 5, 2022, Pope Francis published a chirograph with the appointment of an inter-dicasterial commission with the task of adapting and modifying the *Regolamento generale della Curia romana* in light of *Praedicate Evangelium*, and to advise about the conformity and updating of the *Ordines servandi* and/or "Statutes" of all institutions of the Roman Curia.[68]

This step—from the apostolic constitution to the statutes of individual dicasteries and other institutions of the Roman Curia—will be very important because the new apostolic constitution is one of the most important legislative acts that Francis has promulgated since his election in 2013. But it is still too early to say whether *Praedicate Evangelium* fundamentally changes the Roman Curia like the reforms of 1588 (after Trent), 1908 (after the fall of the Papal States), and 1967 (after Vatican II) did. A lot will depend on the statutes of individual dicasteries and the people who are hired to work there at all levels. It will also depend on the kind of bishops that will be appointed around the world and who will have to interact with the Curia from their dioceses and bishops' conferences.

Praedicate Evangelium comes at a time that is reminiscent of that transitionary period in the first half of the nineteenth century. It followed the storm of the French Revolution, the French occupations of Rome, and lasted until 1870 with the

68. Members of the commission: Msgr. Filippo Iannone, OCarm, President of the Pontifical Council for Legislative Texts; Msgr. Edgar Peña Parra, substitute for the general affairs of the Secretariat of State; Msgr. Nunzio Galantino, President of the APSA (Amministrazione del Patrimonio della Sede Apostolica); Fr. Juan Antonio Guerrero Alves, SJ, Prefect of the Secretariat for the Economy; Prof. Vincenzo Buonomo, Rettore of the Pontifical Lateran University; Msgr. Marco Mellino, secretary of the commission.

fall of the Papal States, which, in the history of the Curia, was a change even more consequential than Vatican II because the loss of temporal power of the pope had made superfluous many offices and institutions.

But there is no doubt that *Praedicate Evangelium* is a reform of the Roman Curia typical of the postconciliar Church. On the one hand, it is a serious effort to shape the Curia according to the ecclesiology of Vatican II and reflective of a less Italian, less European, and more global Church. On the other hand, it encompasses all the uncertainties of Catholic theology about institutions, still trying to find a balance between the *urbs* (Rome) and the *orbis* (the Church in the world), papal primacy and episcopacy, the bureaucratic and the charismatic. It also reflects the uneasy relationship, if not alienation, in the Catholic Church between theology, magisterium, and canon law, and some of the hesitations of Pope Francis as a legislator.[69]

It is interesting to see that this reform has been published in the middle of the "synodal process" rather than afterward. But evidently it was also a priority to publish this apostolic constitution before the end of the pontificate and before the conclave electing the successor of Francis. Remarkably, *Praedicate Evangelium* has been published with Benedict XVI still alive, more than nine years after his resignation, and the constitution does not address the issue of the institution of the "pope emeritus."

There are some positive tensions and possible contradictions. Synodality is a key concept for Francis's pontificate, but

69. On this see the important book by the Italian canon lawyer Geraldina Boni, *La recente attività normativa ecclesiale: finis terrae per lo ius canonicum? Per una valorizzazione del ruolo del Pontificio Consiglio per i testi legislativi e della scienza nella Chiesa* (Modena: Mucchi, 2021).

the foundations of the Roman Curia in the Middle Ages were based on a "consistorial system" of meetings of cardinals deciding in a collegial way, which was in place before the modern concept of permanent congregations or dicasteries. It was, to some extent, a system of government more "collegial" than the one that was created in 1588, where everyone became accountable to the pope but in a system of silos. The Curia that is envisioned and mapped out by *Praedicate Evangelium* may become less Roman (the term "bishops' conferences" is used fifty-eight times) and less clerical (the possibility of appointing lay leaders of dicasteries). But it is also a more papal Curia.

This document must be read in the context of Francis's distance from the Curia, which is not just a matter of words, but also of a style of governing the Church. Francis governs mostly without the Curia, but he has not disbanded them. At the same time, he has articulated a vision of the future of the Roman Curia as "the antenna" of the global Catholic Church—a receiving and transmitting antenna. On the other hand, this reform of the Curia will take effect in the context of a college of cardinals that is more globally diverse than ever. Individually, many of today's cardinals are theologically and spiritually closer to Francis, but they are also more physically and culturally distant from Rome. This will have an impact on the way the Roman Curia behaves toward the Church of the "peripheries" and vice versa.

The Curia has changed in history, but many of those changes happened not just because of theological ideas or Church power struggles, but also because of world events: wars (in Europe in the nineteenth century), financial crises (such as the Great Depression of 1929 and its financial effects, which were also felt in Rome), decolonization (no less influential than Vatican II). In this sense, it is interesting that the possible diminution of the role of the Secretary of State takes place at a moment when, because of the war in Ukraine and the disruption of the international order, its role of coordination and assistance to the pope is more important than it was in 2013, when discussions on a new apostolic constitution began.

Only with the passage of time will we be able to see if the real effects of *Praedicate Evangelium* can live up to the expectations of a new order of things in the Catholic Church. The real problem of the Curia and its irreformability or resistance to reform has always been much less the Curia itself than the Roman court. In the centuries before 1870, the court of the king pope absorbed the Curia. But even since the power of the pope as a sovereign over a real territory and state disappeared, the Roman court around the pope has still continued to exist: court in the sense of those spaces (embassies of foreign countries and international organizations to the Holy See, cultural and academic institutions, circles and think tanks, NGOs and advocacy groups, restaurants and villas) for the socializing that is necessary for initiating and conducting the "political" negotiations that are part of the work of every bureaucracy—including the Vatican. These days, there is also a new court, made of the media and social media court, without which the papacy cannot operate effectively in the global world. *Praedicate Evangelium* legislates on the Roman Curia, but it can also connect in new ways the Roman court, the Roman Curia, and an extraordinarily diverse Catholic Church around the world. It would be one of the long-term effects of Vatican II.

Massimo Faggioli

POPE FRANCIS

APOSTOLIC CONSTITUTION

PRAEDICATE EVANGELIUM

on the Roman Curia and Its Service
to the Church in the World

I.
PREAMBLE

1. *Praedicate Evangelium* (cf. *Mk* 16:15; *Mt* 10:7-8): this is the task that the Lord Jesus entrusted to his disciples. This mandate constitutes "the primary service that the Church can render to every individual and to all humanity in the modern world".[1] To this end, she has been called to proclaim the Gospel of the Son of God, Christ the Lord, and thereby to awaken in all peoples the hearing of faith (*Rom* 1:1-5; *Gal* 3:5). The Church carries out this command above all when, in all that she says and does, she bears witness to the mercy that she herself has graciously received. Our Lord and Master left us an example of this when he washed the feet of his disciples and declared that we shall be blessed if we do likewise (cf. *Jn* 13:14-17). "An evangelizing community thus gets involved by word and deed in people's daily lives, it bridges distances, it is willing to abase itself if necessary and it embraces human life, touching the suffering flesh of Christ in others".[2] In this way, the people of God fulfils the commandment of the Lord who, in bidding us to proclaim the Gospel, exhorted us to care for those of our brothers and sisters who are most vulnerable, infirm and suffering.

Missionary conversion of the Church

2. The Church's "missionary conversion"[3] aims to renew her as a mirror of Christ's own mission of love. The Lord's disciples are called to be "the light of the world" (*Mt* 5:14). In this way, the Church reflects the saving love of Christ, the true light of the world (cf. *Jn* 8:12). She herself becomes increasingly radiant as she brings to humanity the supernatural gift of faith as "a light for our way, guiding our journey through time". The Church is at the service of the Gospel, so that "this light of faith . . . can grow and illumine the present, becoming a star to brighten the horizon of our journey at a time when mankind is particularly in need of light".[4]

3. The reform of the Roman Curia is to be viewed in the context of the Church's missionary nature. The desire for reform was urgently felt in the sixteenth century, leading to the Apostolic Constitution *Immensa Aeterni Dei* of Sixtus V (1588), and in the twentieth century, leading to the Apostolic Constitution *Sapienti Consilio* of Pius X (1908). Following the Second Vatican Council, Paul VI, with explicit reference to the desire expressed by the Council Fathers,[5] called for and carried out a reform of the Curia with the Apostolic Constitution *Regimini Ecclesiae Universae* (1967). Subsequently, in 1988, John Paul II promulgated the Apostolic Constitution *Pastor Bonus*, with the aim of further promoting communion within the Church's overall structures.

In continuity with these two recent reforms, and with appreciation for the longstanding, generous and competent service to the Roman Pontiff and the universal Church provided by so many members of the Curia, this new Apostolic Constitution seeks to attune its present-day activity more effectively to the path of evangelization that the Church, especially in our time, has taken.

The Church: a mystery of communion

4. The reform of the Roman Curia demands attention to, and appreciation for, yet another aspect of the mystery of the Church. In her, mission and communion are so closely united that we can say that the purpose of mission is precisely that of "making everyone know and live the 'new' communion that the Son of God made man has introduced into the history of the world".[6]

This life of communion makes the Church *synodal*; a Church marked by reciprocal listening, "whereby everyone has something to learn. The faithful people, the College of Bishops, the Bishop of Rome: all listening to each other and all listening to the Holy Spirit, the Spirit of truth (cf. *Jn* 14:17), in order to know what he says to the Churches (cf. *Rev* 2:7)".[7] This synodal nature of the Church is to be understood as "the journeying together of God's flock along the paths of history towards the encounter with Christ the Lord".[8] It has to do with the mission of the Church and the communion that is in service to that mission and is itself missionary.

The renewal of the Church, and consequently of the Roman Curia, cannot fail to reflect this basic reciprocity, so that the community of believers can approximate as much as possible the missionary communion experienced by the Apostles with the Lord during his earthly life (cf. *Mk* 3:14) and, after Pentecost, by the first community of Jerusalem, guided by the Holy Spirit (cf. *Acts* 2:42).

Service of the Primacy and of the College of Bishops

5. Outstanding among these gifts bestowed by the Spirit for the service of humanity is that of the Apostles, whom the Lord chose and established as a stable group (*coetus*) over whom he set Peter, chosen from among them, as their head.[9] He entrusted to the Apostles a mission that will endure until the end of time. For this reason, they took care to appoint successors,[10] so that, just as Peter and the other Apostles constituted, by the will of the Lord, one apostolic college, so today, in the Church, as a hierarchically organized society,[11] the Roman Pontiff, the successor of Peter, and the Bishops, the successors of the Apostles, are joined together in a single episcopal body, to which Bishops belong in virtue of sacramental consecration and by hierarchical communion with the head of the college and its members, that is, with the college itself.[12]

6. As the Second Vatican Council teaches: "Collegial unity is also apparent in the mutual relations of individual Bishops to particular dioceses and to the universal Church. The Roman Pontiff, as the successor of Peter, is the perpetual and visible source and foundation of unity both of the Bishops and of the whole company of the faithful. Individual Bishops are the visible source and foundation of unity in their own particular Churches, which are modelled on the universal Church; it is in and from these that the one and unique Catholic Church exists. For that reason, each Bishop represents his own Church, whereas all of them together with the Pope represent the whole Church in a bond of peace love and unity".[13]

7. It must be emphasized that, by God's providence, over the course of time various Churches were founded in different

places by the Apostles and by their successors, and have come together in diverse groupings, chiefly the ancient patriarchal Churches. The emergence of Episcopal Conferences in the Latin Church represents one of the more recent forms in which the *communio Episcoporum* has found expression in service to the *communio Ecclesiae* grounded in the *communio fidelium*. Consequently, while fully respecting the proper power of each Bishop as pastor of the particular Church entrusted to him, Episcopal Conferences, including their regional and continental groupings, together with the relative hierarchical structures of the Eastern Churches, are presently one of the most significant means for expressing and preserving ecclesial communion in different places, together with the Roman Pontiff as guarantor of unity of faith and of communion.[14]

Service of the Roman Curia

8. The Roman Curia is at the service of the Pope, who, as the successor of Peter, is the perpetual and visible source and foundation of the unity both of the Bishops and of the whole company of the faithful.[15] By virtue of this bond, the work of the Roman Curia is also organically related to the College of Bishops and individual Bishops, as well as to Episcopal Conferences and their regional and continental groupings, and the hierarchical structures of the Eastern Churches. All these are of great pastoral benefit as expressions of the affective and effective communion existing among the Bishops. The Roman Curia is not set between the Pope and the Bishops, but is at the service of both, according to the modalities proper to the nature of each.

9. The attention that the present Apostolic Constitution gives to Episcopal Conferences and, correspondingly, to the hierarchical structures of the Eastern Churches, is meant to enhance their potential,[16] without making them intermediary instances between the Roman Pontiff and the Bishops, but instead being at their complete service. The competencies assigned to them in the present provisions are meant to express the collegial dimension of the episcopal ministry and, indirectly, to strengthen ecclesial communion[17] by giving concrete expression to their joint exercise of certain pastoral functions for the good of the faithful of their respective nations or of a determined territory.[18]

Every Christian is a missionary disciple

10. The Pope, the Bishops and other ordained ministers are not the sole evangelizers in the Church. They "know that they were not established by Christ to undertake by themselves the entire saving mission of the Church to the world".[19] Each Christian, by virtue of baptism, is a missionary disciple "to the extent that he or she has encountered the love of God in Christ Jesus".[20] This must necessarily be taken into account in the reform of the Curia, which should consequently make provision for the involvement of lay women and men, also in roles of government and responsibility. Their presence and their participation is essential, since they contribute to the well-being of the entire Church.[21] By their family life, their engagement in society and their faith, which helps them to discern God's working in the world, they have much to offer, especially through their promotion of the family, respect for the values of life and creation, the Gospel as a leaven of temporal affairs, and the discernment of the signs of the times.

Significance of the reform

11. The reform of the Roman Curia will be authentic and effective if it is the fruit of an interior reform whereby we appropriate "the paradigm of the spirituality of the Council" as expressed in "the ancient story of the good Samaritan",[22] the person who goes out of his way to be a neighbour to someone left half-dead on the roadside, a foreigner whom he does not even know. This spirituality has its deepest source in the love of God, who loved us first, while we were still poor sinners. It reminds us that our duty is, in imitation of Christ, to serve our brothers and sisters, especially those in greatest need, and that Christ's face is seen in the face of every man and woman, particularly those who suffer in any way (cf. *Mt* 25:40).

12. It should therefore be evident that "reform is not an end in itself, but a means to give a more convincing witness to Christ; to favour a more effective evangelization; to promote a more fruitful ecumenical spirit; to encourage a more constructive dialogue with all. This reform, actively endorsed by most Cardinals within the General Congregations prior to the Conclave, should further clarify the identity of the Roman Curia in the assistance it provides to the successor of Peter in the exercise of his supreme pastoral office for the benefit and service of the universal Church and the particular Churches. This entails strengthening the unity of faith and the communion of the people of God and advancing the mission of the Church in the world. Certainly, it will not be easy to achieve this goal: it will require time, determination and, above all, the cooperation of everyone. To do so, we must first of all entrust ourselves to the Holy Spirit, who is the true guide of the Church, and implore in prayer the gift of authentic discernment".[23]

II.
PRINCIPLES AND CRITERIA
FOR THE SERVICE OF
THE ROMAN CURIA

To carry out effectively the pastoral mission of solicitude for the entire Church that the Roman Pontiff has received from Christ, her Lord and Pastor (cf. *Jn* 21:15ff.), and to preserve and foster the relationship existing between the Petrine ministry and the ministry of all the Bishops, the Pope, "in exercising his supreme, full and immediate authority over the universal Church, employs the various departments of the Roman Curia, which act in his name and by his authority for the good of the Churches and in the service of the sacred pastors".[24] The Curia is thus at the service of the Pope and of the Bishops, who, "together with Peter's successor . . . govern the house of the living God".[25] The Curia exercises this service to the Bishops in their particular Churches with due respect for their responsibilities as successors of the Apostles.

1. **Service to the mission of the Pope**. The Roman Curia is primarily an instrument at the service of the successor

of Peter to assist him in his mission as "perpetual and visible source and foundation of the unity both of the Bishops and of the whole company of the faithful",[26] and to be of assistance to Bishops, particular Churches, Episcopal Conferences and their regional and continental groupings, the hierarchical structures of the Eastern Churches and other institutions and communities in the Church.

2. **Co-responsibility in** *communio*. The present reform proposes, in the spirit of a "sound decentralization",[27] to leave to the competence of Bishops the authority to resolve, in the exercise of "their proper task as teachers" and pastors,[28] those issues with which they are familiar[29] and that do not affect the Church's unity of doctrine, discipline and communion, always acting with that spirit of co-responsibility which is the fruit and expression of the specific *mysterium communionis* that is the Church.[30]

3. **Service to the mission of the Bishops**. In this context of cooperation with the Bishops, the service that the Curia offers them consists primarily in acknowledging and supporting their ministry to the Gospel and the Church. It does so by providing them with timely counsel, encouraging the pastoral conversion that they promote, showing solidary support for their efforts at evangelization, their preferential pastoral option for the poor, their protection of minors and vulnerable persons, and all their initiatives to serve the human family, unity and peace. In a word, the Curia backs their efforts to enable the peoples to have abundant life in Christ. The Curia also offers its service to the mission of Bishops and to *communio* by carrying out, in a fraternal spirit, tasks of vigilance, support and enhancement of the

affective and effective communion of the successor of Peter with the Bishops.

4. **Support for the particular Churches and their Episcopal Conferences and for the hierarchical structures of the Eastern Churches**. The Catholic Church throughout the world embraces a multitude of peoples, languages and cultures, and thus can draw upon an immense store of successful experiences regarding evangelization; this must not be lost. Based on the Church's presence worldwide, the Roman Curia, in its service to the good of the entire *communio*, is in a position to draw upon and process this rich fund of knowledge and the fruits of the best initiatives and creative proposals for evangelization devised by individual particular Churches, Episcopal Conferences and the hierarchical structures of the Eastern Churches, as well as their responses to specific problems and challenges. By assembling these experiences of the Church in her universality, the Curia can share them, by way of support, with the particular Churches, the Episcopal Conferences and the hierarchical structures of the Eastern Churches. For this kind of exchange and dialogue, the visits of the Bishops *ad limina Apostolorum* and their relative reports represent an important resource.

5. **The vicarious nature of the Roman Curia**. Each curial institution carries out its proper mission by virtue of the power it has received from the Roman Pontiff, in whose name it operates with vicarious power in the exercise of his primatial *munus*. For this reason, any member of the faithful can preside over a Dicastery or Office, depending on the power of governance and the specific competence and function of the Dicastery or Office in question.

6. **Spirituality**. The Roman Curia contributes to the Church's communion with the Lord solely by cultivating the relationship of all its members with Christ Jesus, working generously and fervently in service to God's plan, the gifts that the Holy Spirit bestows on the Church, and the vocation of all the baptized to holiness. It is necessary, therefore, that in each institution of the Curia, service to the Church as mystery remains joined to an experience of the covenant with God, manifested by common prayer, spiritual renewal and periodic common celebrations of the Eucharist. In the same way, based on their encounter with Jesus Christ, the members of the Curia are to carry out their work in the joyful recognition that they are missionary disciples at the service of the entire people of God.

7. **Personal integrity and professionalism**. The face of Christ is reflected in the varied faces of those of his disciples who place their charisms at the service of the Church's mission. Consequently, those who serve in the Curia are chosen from Bishops, priests, deacons, members of Institutes of Consecrated Life and Societies of Apostolic Life, and lay men and women outstanding for their spiritual life, solid pastoral experience, simplicity of life and love for the poor, spirit of communion and service, competence in the matters entrusted to them, and ability to discern the signs of the times. For this reason, care and attention must be given to the selection and training of personnel, as well as the organization of work and the personal and professional growth of every individual.

8. **Cooperation between Dicasteries**. Communion and participation must be the hallmark of the internal working

of the Curia and each of its institutions. The Roman Curia must increasingly be at the service of communion of life and operational unity around the pastors of the universal Church. Superiors of Dicasteries thus meet periodically with the Roman Pontiff, both individually and in groups. These periodic meetings favour transparency and concerted action in discussing the work plans of the Dicasteries and their application.

9. **Interdicasterial and intradicasterial meetings**. Interdicasterial meetings, which express the communion and cooperation existing within the Curia, discuss matters involving more than one Dicastery. Responsibility for convening these meetings belongs to the Secretariat of State, since it acts as the Papal Secretariat. Communion and cooperation are also shown by appropriate periodic meetings of the members of each individual Dicastery: plenary sessions, consultations and congresses. This spirit must also mark the meetings of Bishops with the Dicasteries, whether individually or in groups, as on the occasion of their visits *ad limina Apostolorum*.

10. **Expression of catholicity**. The catholicity of the Church must be expressed in the selection of Cardinals, Bishops and other personnel. All those invited to serve in the Roman Curia are a sign of communion and solidarity with the Roman Pontiff on the part of the Bishops and Superiors of Institutes of Consecrated Life and Societies of Apostolic Life who make available to the Roman Curia qualified personnel coming from different cultures.

11. Reduction of Dicasteries. It has been necessary to reduce the number of the Dicasteries, unifying those whose purpose was very similar or complementary, and streamlining their functions with the aim of avoiding an overlap of competencies and improving the effectiveness of their work.

12. The chief aim of reform, as desired by Paul VI, is to allow the spark of God's love to kindle, in the Curia and the entire Church, "the principles, teachings and resolves set forth by the Council, so that, fanned into flame by charity, they might truly bring about, in the Church and in the world, that renewal of mind, action, conduct, moral conviction, hope and joy which was the ultimate purpose of the Council".[31]

III.
GENERAL NORMS

Notion of the Roman Curia

Art. 1

The Roman Curia is the institution that ordinarily assists the Roman Pontiff in exercising his supreme pastoral office and universal mission in the world. It is at the service of the Pope, the successor of Peter, and of the Bishops, successors of the Apostles, in ways that correspond to each one's specific nature. It carries out its function with evangelical spirit, working for the good and service of communion, unity and the building up of the universal Church, while also attentive to the circumstances of the world in which the Church is called to carry out its mission.

The Pastoral Nature of the Work of the Curia

Art. 2

Since all the members of the people of God, each according to his or her own condition, take part in the mission of the Church, those who serve in the Roman Curia cooperate in a way that corresponds to their expertise and competence, as well as to their pastoral experience.

Art. 3

Those who work in the Roman Curia and other institutions associated with the Holy See carry out a pastoral service in support of the mission of the Roman Pontiff and of the Bishops in their respective responsibilities with regard to the universal Church. This service must be motivated and carried out with the highest sense of cooperation, shared responsibility and respect for the competence of others.

Art. 4

The pastoral character of curial service is nourished and enriched by a particular spirituality rooted in the relationship of mutual interiority that exists between the universal Church and the particular Church.

Art. 5

The distinct nature of the Roman Curia's pastoral service demands that everyone recognize the call to an exemplary life in the Church and in the world. This entails everyone's engagement in the demanding task of being missionary disciples, showing an example of dedication, a spirit of piety, of welcome to those who come to them, and of service.

Art. 6

Along with the service provided in the Roman Curia, clerics should also attend to the care of souls whenever possible and without prejudice to their work in the office. The members of Institutes of Consecrated Life and Societies of Apostolic Life and the laity should collaborate in the pastoral activities of their own communities or other ecclesial realities according to each one's abilities and opportunities.

The Operating Principles of the Roman Curia

Art. 7

§1. For the proper functioning of each component of the Roman Curia, it is essential that, in addition to their dedication and virtue, those who work there should have the necessary qualifications. This requires professionalism, that is, possession of the expertise and ability to handle competently the matters assigned to them. Although this is acquired and developed with time, through experience, study and self-improvement, it is necessary, however, that the individual be adequately prepared from the outset.

§2. The different components of the Roman Curia, each according to its nature and competence, should provide ongoing formation for their staff.

Art. 8

§1. The activity of each component of the Roman Curia must always be inspired by the criteria of reasonableness and functionality, in response to situations that arise over time and the needs of the universal Church and of the particular Churches.

§2. Functionality, which is aimed at offering the best and most effective service, requires that all those who work in the Roman Curia always be ready to carry out their work when needed.

Art. 9

§1. In carrying out its particular service, each Dicastery, Institution or Office is called, by reason of the mission in which it shares, to fulfil this service through cooperation with other Dicasteries, Institutions or Offices in a spirit of mutual collaboration, each according to its own competence, in continual interdependence and interconnection of activities.

§2. This cooperation is also fostered within each Dicastery, Institution or Office by the individual who carries out his or her work in such a way that each person's diligence fosters the building up of an orderly and effective functioning, which transcends cultural, linguistic and national differences.

§3. The provisions of §§1-2 especially apply to the Secretariat of State since it is the Papal Secretariat.

Art. 10
In carrying out its work, each Dicastery, Institution or Office makes regular and appropriate use of the specific means envisioned in this Apostolic Constitution, such as the congress, in ordinary or plenary sessions. Interdicasterial meetings and meetings of heads of Dicasteries should also be held regularly.

Art. 11
Everything that concerns the performance of the personnel of the Roman Curia and other related issues falls within the competence of the Labour Office of the Apostolic See, whose duty it is to protect and promote the rights of collaborators, according to the principles of the social doctrine of the Church.

The Structure of the Roman Curia

Art. 12
§1. The Roman Curia is composed of the Secretariat of State, the Dicasteries and other Institutions, all juridically equal among themselves.

§2. The expression "curial institutions" is understood to mean the various components of the Roman Curia referred to in §1.

§3. Among the Offices of the Roman Curia are the Prefecture of the Papal Household, the Office for the Liturgical Celebrations of the Supreme Pontiff and the Camerlengo of the Holy Roman Church.

Art. 13

§1. Each curial institution has a Prefect, or equivalent, an adequate number of members, including one or more Secretaries who assist the Prefect, together with, but subordinately, one or more Undersecretaries, all of whom are assisted by various officials and consultors.

§2. Depending on its particular nature, or a special law, a curial institution can have a structure other than the one established in §1.

Art. 14

§1. The curial institution is governed by the Prefect, or equivalent, who heads it and acts in its name.

§2. The Secretary, with the help of the Undersecretary or Undersecretaries, assists the Prefect in handling the work of the Dicastery as well as directing the personnel.

§3. The officials are selected, as far as possible, from various regions of the world, so that the Curia may reflect the universal character of the Church. They are taken from among clerics, members of Institutes of Consecrated Life and Societies of Apostolic Life and the laity, who are distinguished for their experience, proven expertise attested by appropriate academic degrees, virtue and prudence. They should be chosen by objective and transparent criteria, and should have a suitable number of years of pastoral experience.

§4. The suitability of the applicants should be ascertained by appropriate means.

§5. In choosing clerics as officials, care should be taken, as far as possible, to maintain a balance between diocesan or eparchial clerics and those of Institutes of Consecrated Life and Societies of Apostolic Life.

Art. 15

The members of curial institutions are appointed from among the Cardinals living in Rome or outside the city, to whom are added some Bishops, especially diocesan or eparchial ones, insofar as they have expertise in the particular matters involved. Depending on the nature of the Dicastery, priests, deacons, those in Institutes of Consecrated Life and Societies of Apostolic Life and lay faithful may also be appointed members.

Art. 16

The consultors of curial institutions and offices are appointed from among the faithful who are distinguished by their expertise, proven ability and prudence. In identifying and choosing them, care must be taken to respect, as much as possible, the criterion of universality.

Art. 17

§1. The Prefect, or equivalent, the members, the Secretary, the Undersecretary and other senior officials who are heads of office, their equivalents and experts, as well as consultors, are appointed by the Roman Pontiff for a five-year term.

§2. The Prefect and the Secretary, having reached the age provided for by the *General Regulations of the Roman Curia*, must submit their resignation to the Roman Pontiff, who, after considering all factors, will make a determination in this regard.

§3. Members who have reached eighty years of age cease from their appointment. However, those who hold a position in a curial institution also cease to be members when they no longer hold that position.

§4. As a rule, after five years, clerical officials and members of Institutes of Consecrated Life and Societies of Apostolic Life who have served in curial institutions and offices are to return to their Diocese or Eparchy, or to the Institute or Society to which they belong to continue their pastoral work. If the Superiors of the Roman Curia deem it appropriate, their service can be extended for another five-year period.

Art. 18

§1. When the Apostolic See is vacant, all heads of curial institutions and members cease from their office. Those exempt from this rule are the Major Penitentiary, who continues to carry out the ordinary business within his competence and refers all matters to the College of Cardinals which otherwise would have been referred to the Roman Pontiff, and the Almoner of His Holiness, who continues to exercise the works of charity, according to the same criteria followed during the Pontificate and remains at the service of the College of the Cardinals until the election of the new Roman Pontiff.

§2. When the See is vacant, the Secretaries attend to the ordinary governance of curial institutions, taking care of ordinary business only. They must be confirmed in office by the Roman Pontiff within three months of his election.

§3. The Master of Pontifical Liturgical Celebrations assumes the duties provided for by the law concerning the vacancy of the Apostolic See and the election of the Roman Pontiff.

Art. 19
Each of the curial institutions and offices is to maintain its own archive in which incoming documents and copies of outgoing documents are protocolled and kept safe and in good order, according to appropriate criteria.

Competencies and Procedures of Curial Institutions

Art. 20
The competence of curial institutions is normally determined on the basis of subject matter. However, it is possible that competencies may also be established for other reasons.

Art. 21
Each curial institution, depending on its proper area of competence:

1. deals with those matters which, either by their nature or by law, are reserved to the Apostolic See;

2. deals with matters entrusted to it by the Roman Pontiff;

3. examines those matters that exceed the competence of individual diocesan or eparchial Bishops or episcopal bodies (Conferences or hierarchical structures of the Eastern Churches);

4. studies the major problems of the current age, so that the Church's pastoral activity may be more effectively promoted and suitably coordinated, always with respect and due regard for the competencies of the particular Churches, Episcopal

Conferences, regional and continental groupings, as well as the hierarchical structures of Eastern Churches;

5. promotes, favours and encourages initiatives and proposals for the good of the universal Church;

6. evaluates and, if necessary, decides those matters that the faithful, exercising their right, refer directly to the Apostolic See.

Art. 22

Possible conflicts of competencies arising among Dicasteries or between Dicasteries and the Secretariat of State are to be submitted to the Supreme Tribunal of the Apostolic Signatura, unless the Roman Pontiff determines otherwise.

Art. 23

Each curial institution addresses matters within its competence in accordance with universal law, the special law of the Roman Curia and its proper norms, applying the law always with canonical equity, attentive both to justice and the good of the Church, and, especially, to the salvation of souls.

Art. 24

The heads of curial institutions or, in their stead, the Secretaries, are received by the Roman Pontiff, in the manner established by him, in order to report regularly and frequently on current matters, activities and programmes.

Art. 25

It is the responsibility of the head of the Dicastery, unless otherwise specified for individual Dicasteries, to convoke the congress, composed of the head of the Dicastery, the

Secretary, the Undersecretary and, in the judgment of the head of the Dicastery, all or some of the officials:

1. to examine specific matters and identify their resolution by a prompt decision, or by referring them to the ordinary or plenary session or to an interdicasterial meeting, or by presenting them to the Roman Pontiff;

2. to present to the consultors or other experts the matters that require particular study;

3. to examine requests for faculties and rescripts, according to the competencies of the Dicastery.

Art. 26

§1. The members of the Dicasteries meet in ordinary and plenary sessions.

§2. For ordinary sessions, concerning normal or regular matters, it is sufficient to convoke members of the Dicastery who reside in Rome.

§3. All the members of the Dicastery are convoked for the plenary session. It is to be held every two years, unless the *Ordo servandus* of the Dicastery determines a longer period of time, and always after the Roman Pontiff has been informed. Matters and questions of greater importance are reserved for the plenary session, according to the nature of the Dicastery. It is convoked, as needed, to deal also with matters of general principle or others that the head of the Dicastery deems necessary to address in this manner.

§4. In planning the work of the sessions, especially the plenary sessions that require the presence of all members, efforts should be made to limit the necessity of travel through use of videoconferences and other means of communication that are sufficiently confidential and secure to allow for effective collaboration independent of the need for being physically present in the same place.

§5. The Secretary participates in all the sessions with the right to vote.

Art. 27
§1. The consultors and those equivalent to them are to study the matter entrusted to them and to present their opinion, generally in writing.

§2. When deemed necessary and according to the specific nature of the Dicastery, the consultors – all or some of them, given their specific competencies – can be called together to examine particular matters in a collegial fashion and give their opinion.

§3. In individual cases, persons not counted among the consultors and who are noted for their special competence and experience in the particular matter to be addressed can be invited to offer advice.

Art. 28
§1. Matters touching the competence of more than one Dicastery are to be examined together by the Dicasteries concerned.

§2. The head of the Dicastery to which the matter was first referred convenes the meeting either on his own initiative or at the request of another Dicastery concerned, to examine the various points of view and come to a decision.

§3. In the event that the subject matter requires it, the question must be referred to a joint plenary session of the Dicasteries involved.

§4. The meeting will be presided over by the head of the Dicastery who convoked the meeting or by the Secretary, if only Secretaries are participating.

§5. When deemed necessary, in order to deal with matters requiring mutual and frequent consultation, the head of the Dicastery that has begun to deal with the matter or to whom the matter was first referred, establishes a special interdicasterial commission with the prior approval of the Roman Pontiff.

Art. 29

§1. The curial institution that prepares a general document, before submitting it to the Roman Pontiff, will send it to other interested curial institutions, in order to receive possible observations, amendments and suggestions for improvement so that through different perspectives and evaluations, a unified implementation of the document can be achieved.

§2. Documents or statements on matters relating to relations with States and with other subjects of international law require the prior *nihil obstat* of the Secretariat of State.

Art. 30

A curial institution cannot issue laws or general decrees having the force of law, nor can it derogate from the prescriptions of the current universal law, except in individual and particular cases, and with the approval of the Roman Pontiff *in forma specifica*.

Art. 31

§1. It is a binding norm that nothing grave and extraordinary be transacted unless the Roman Pontiff be previously informed by the head of a curial institution.

§2. Decisions and resolutions concerning matters of major importance must be submitted for the approval of the Roman Pontiff, except decisions for which special faculties have been granted to curial institutions as well as sentences of the Tribunal of the Roman Rota and the Supreme Tribunal of the Apostolic Signatura issued within the limits of their proper competence.

§3. With regard to special faculties granted to a curial institution, the Prefect or his equivalent is required to examine and evaluate periodically with the Roman Pontiff their effectiveness, viability, implementation within the Roman Curia and suitability for the universal Church.

Art. 32

§1. Hierarchical recourses are received, examined and decided, in accordance with the law, by the curial institution that has competence in that subject matter. In case of doubt with regard to the determination of competence, the Supreme Tribunal of the Apostolic Signatura resolves the question.

§2. Matters that must be dealt with juridically are sent to the competent Tribunals.

Art. 33

The curial institutions cooperate, according to their respective specific competencies, in the work of the General Secretariat of the Synod, paying attention to what is established in the specific legislation of the Synod itself, which collaborates with the Roman Pontiff, in accordance with the methods established or to be established by him, in matters of major importance for the good of the whole Church.

Meeting of Heads of Curial Institutions

Art. 34

§1. In order to foster greater coherence and transparency in the work of the Curia, by mandate of the Roman Pontiff, the heads of curial institutions are regularly convened to discuss the work plans of each institution and their implementation; to coordinate shared tasks; to give and receive information and examine matters of major importance; to offer opinions and suggestions; and to make decisions to be presented to the Roman Pontiff.

§2. The meetings are convened and coordinated by the Secretary of State in agreement with the Roman Pontiff.

Art. 35

If the Roman Pontiff deems it appropriate, more serious business of a general character, already under discussion in the meeting of the heads of the curial institutions, can also be dealt with by the Cardinals assembled in Consistory according to proper law.

The Roman Curia at the Service of the Particular Churches

Art. 36

§1. In more serious matters, curial institutions must cooperate with the particular Churches, the Episcopal Conferences, their regional and continental groupings and the hierarchical structures of the Eastern Churches.

§2. When the matter requires, documents of a general nature of major importance or those which concern in a special way some particular Churches, are to be prepared taking into account the opinion of the Episcopal Conferences, their regional and continental groupings, and the hierarchical structures of the Eastern Churches concerned.

§3. Curial institutions should quickly acknowledge receipt of the requests presented to them by the particular Churches, examine them diligently and promptly and provide an appropriate response as soon as possible.

Art. 37

With regard to matters concerning particular Churches, curial institutions should consult the Pontifical Representatives who carry out their function in that place and should not fail to inform them, the Episcopal Conferences and the hierarchical structures of the Eastern Churches about the decisions taken.

Ad limina Apostolorum *Visits*

Art. 38

In keeping with the tradition and the prescriptions of canon law, the Pastors of each particular Church make the *ad limina Apostolorum* visit at predetermined times.

Art. 39

This visit has a particular importance for the unity and communion in the life of the Church, inasmuch it constitutes the summit of the relationship of the Pastors of each particular Church, each Episcopal Conference and each hierarchical structure of the Eastern Churches with the Bishop of Rome. Indeed, in receiving his brothers in the Episcopate, he deals with them about matters concerning the good of Churches and the pastoral function of the Bishops, and he confirms and supports them in faith and charity. In this way, the bonds of hierarchical communion are strengthened and both the catholicity of the Church and the unity of the College of Bishops are made clear.

Art. 40

§1. The Pastors of each particular Church called to participate in the visit must prepare for it with care and diligence, submitting to the Apostolic See at the times indicated a detailed report on the state of the Diocese or Eparchy entrusted to them, including a report on its financial and patrimonial situation.

§2. The report should be concise and clear and should be characterized by precision and concreteness in describing the real condition of the particular Church. It must also contain an evaluation of the support received from curial institutions and articulate expectations concerning the work to be accomplished in cooperation with the Curia.

§3. To facilitate the discussions, the Pastors of the particular Churches should attach a summary of the main themes to the detailed report.

Art. 41

The visit is divided into three principal moments: the pilgrimage to the tombs of the Princes of the Apostles, the meeting with the Roman Pontiff and the discussions with the Dicasteries and Institutions of Justice of the Roman Curia.

Art. 42

§1. The Prefects or their equivalents, and the respective Secretaries of the Dicasteries and Institutions of Justice should prepare diligently for the meeting with the Pastors of particular

Churches, the Episcopal Conferences and the hierarchical structures of the Eastern Churches by carefully examining the reports received from them.

§2. In meeting with the Pastors mentioned in §1, the Prefects or their equivalents, and the respective Secretaries of the Dicasteries and Institutions of Justice, through an open and cordial dialogue, should offer them counsel, encouragement, suggestions and appropriate indications with the aim of contributing to the good and development of the whole Church in observance of the common discipline, and receive suggestions and indications from the Pastors in order to offer an increasingly effective service.

Regulations

Art. 43

§1. Concerning matters of procedure, without prejudice to the prescriptions of the current Codes, the principles and criteria outlined in Part II and the norms laid down in this Apostolic Constitution are to be observed in the *General Regulations of the Roman Curia*, that is, the set of common norms, duly approved by the Roman Pontiff, which establish the order and manner of carrying out work in the Curia and, where expressly provided for, in the Institutions associated with the Holy See.

§2. Each curial institution and office is to have its own *Ordo servandus*, that is, special norms, approved by the Roman Pontiff, according to which its work is carried out.

IV.
SECRETARIAT OF STATE

Art. 44

The Secretariat of State, as the Papal Secretariat, provides close assistance to the Roman Pontiff in the exercise of his supreme mission.

Art. 45

§ 1. It is directed by the Secretary of State.

§ 2. It includes three Sections: the Section for General Affairs, under the direction of the Substitute, assisted by the Assessor; the Section for Relations with States and International Organizations, under the direction of its own Secretary, assisted by the Undersecretary and an Undersecretary for the multilateral sector; and the Section for Diplomatic Personnel of the Holy See, under the direction of the Secretary for Pontifical Representations, assisted by an Undersecretary.

Section for General Affairs

Art. 46

The Section for General Affairs is responsible in a particular way for expediting matters involving the day-to-day service of the Roman Pontiff; examining matters needing to be dealt with outside of the ordinary competence of the institutions of the Curia and the other agencies of the Apostolic See; and fostering cooperation among the Dicasteries, agencies and offices without prejudice to their autonomy. This Section deals with all matters concerning the Representatives of States to the Holy See.

Art. 47

It is also responsible:

1. for drawing up and dispatching apostolic constitutions, decretal letters, apostolic letters, epistles, and other documents entrusted to it by the Roman Pontiff;

2. for preparing for publication the acts and public documents of the Holy See in the official gazette *Acta Apostolicae Sedis*;

3. for giving directions to the Dicastery for Communication regarding official announcements concerning the acts of the Roman Pontiff and the activity of the Holy See;

4. for guarding the lead seal and the Fisherman's ring.

Art. 48

It is likewise the task of this Section:

1. to handle preparations for the periodic meetings of the heads of curial institutions and to enact the decisions made therein;

2. to prepare the appropriate documents concerning appointments made or approved by the Roman Pontiff involving Prefects or their equivalent, members, Secretaries,

Undersecretaries and consultors of curial institutions and offices, and institutions dependent on the Holy See or associated with it, as well as those involving diplomatic personnel;

3. to prepare documentation for the granting of papal honours;

4. to collect, coordinate and publish statistics regarding the life of the Church throughout the world.

Section for Relations with States and International Organizations

Art. 49

The specific task of the Section for Relations with States and International Organizations is to attend to matters dealing with the respective civil authorities.
It is responsible:

1. for fostering the diplomatic and political relations of the Holy See with States and other subjects of international law, and dealing with matters of common interest for the promotion of the good of the Church and of civil society, also by means of concordats and other international agreements, taking account of the considered views of the episcopal bodies that may be affected;

2. for representing the Holy See in international intergovernmental organizations and multilateral intergovernmental conferences, availing itself, when appropriate, of the cooperation of the relevant Dicasteries and Institutions of the Roman Curia;

3. for granting approval whenever a Dicastery or Institution of the Roman Curia intends to publish a statement or a document relating to international affairs or relations with civil authorities.

Art. 50

§ 1. In particular circumstances, this Section, by mandate of the Roman Pontiff and after consultation with the relevant Dicasteries of the Roman Curia, handles all matters concerning the provision of particular Churches, as well as their establishment and any changes made to these and their groupings.

§ 2. In other cases, especially where a concordat is in effect, it is responsible for dealing with matters needing to be treated with civil governments.

Art. 51

§ 1. The Section is assisted by its own council when addressing specific questions.

§ 2. Permanent commissions may be established in the Section whenever necessary for addressing certain matters or general questions concerning different continents and particular geographical areas.

Section for Diplomatic Personnel of the Holy See

Art. 52

§ 1. The Section for Diplomatic Personnel of the Holy See deals with questions concerning persons who serve in the diplomatic service of the Holy See, and in particular their living and working conditions and their ongoing formation. In the fulfilment of his duties, the Secretary makes visits to Papal Representations and convenes and presides at meetings regarding the provision of the same.

§ 2. The Section cooperates with the President of the Pontifical Ecclesiastical Academy concerning the selection and training of candidates for the diplomatic service of the Holy See and maintains contact with retired diplomatic personnel.

§ 3. The Section carries out its responsibilities in close cooperation with the Section for General Affairs and the Section for Relations with States and International Organizations, which, each according to its own specific areas of competence, also deal with matters involving Papal Representatives.

V.
DICASTERIES

Dicastery for Evangelization

Art. 53

§ 1. The Dicastery serves the work of evangelization, so that Christ, the light of the nations, may be known and witnessed to by word and deed, and the Church, his mystical Body, may be built up. The Dicastery is competent for fundamental questions regarding evangelization in the world and for the establishment, assistance and support of new particular Churches, without prejudice to the competence of the Dicastery for the Eastern Churches.

§ 2. The Dicastery is composed of two Sections: the Section for Fundamental Questions regarding Evangelization in the World and the Section for the First Evangelization and New Particular Churches within the territories of its competence.

Art. 54

The Dicastery for Evangelization is presided over directly by the Roman Pontiff. Each of the two Sections is directed in his name and by his authority by a Pro-Prefect, who is assisted in accordance with the norms of Art. 14 § 2.

Section for Fundamental Questions regarding Evangelization in the World

Art. 55

§ 1. It is the task of this Section to study, in cooperation with the particular Churches, Episcopal Conferences and the hierarchical structures of the Eastern Churches, and Institutes of Consecrated Life and Societies of Apostolic Life, fundamental questions regarding evangelization and the development of an effective proclamation of the Gospel, discerning suitable ways, means and language to carry it out. The Section gathers the most significant experiences in the area of evangelization and places them at the disposal of the entire Church.

§ 2. The Section encourages reflection on the history of evangelization and mission, especially in relation to the political, social and cultural contexts that have marked and conditioned the preaching of the Gospel.

Art. 56

§ 1. The Section, through studies and exchanges of experiences, supports the particular Churches in the process of inculturating the Good News of Jesus Christ in different cultures and ethnic groups and the evangelization of the same, with particular attention to popular piety.

§ 2. In promoting and supporting popular piety, it is particularly attentive to international shrines. The Section is competent to erect international shrines and to approve their respective statutes, in conformity with canonical requirements, and, in cooperation with diocesan/eparchial Bishops, Episcopal Conferences and the hierarchical structures of the

Eastern Churches, to promote an organic pastoral care in these shrines, as dynamic centres of continuing evangelization.

Art. 57

In light of political, social and cultural challenges, the Section:

1. promotes evangelization through discernment of the signs of the times and study of the social-economic and environmental conditions of the recipients of the preaching of the Gospel;

2. studies and promotes the renewal that the Gospel brings in its encounter with the various cultures and with all matters concerning the promotion of human dignity and religious freedom. In close cooperation with the particular Churches, Episcopal Conferences and hierarchical structures of the Eastern Churches, it helps and encourages the spread and application of the Church's teaching on the encounter between the Gospel and the various cultures. Since evangelization implies a fundamental option for the poor, it organizes the World Day of the Poor;

3. assists and supports the initiatives of diocesan/eparchial Bishops, Episcopal Conferences and the hierarchical structures of the Eastern Churches for the preaching of the Gospel.

Art. 58

§ 1. The Section is competent for catechesis, placing itself at the service of the particular Churches as they carry out their duty to proclaim the Gospel of Jesus Christ to the baptized in their daily Christian living, to those who show a certain degree of faith but without a sufficient knowledge of its foundations, to those who feel the need to learn more about the teaching they have received, and to those who have abandoned the faith or no longer profess it.

§ 2. The Section exercises vigilance to ensure that religious instruction is properly imparted and catechetical formation carried out in accordance with the norms laid down by the Church's magisterium. It is likewise competent to grant the required confirmation of the Apostolic See for catechisms and other texts relative to catechetical instruction, with the consent of the Dicastery for the Doctrine of the Faith.

Art. 59

§ 1. Since every member of the people of God, by virtue of Baptism, is a missionary disciple of the Gospel, the Section supports the growth of this awareness and responsibility, so that each individual may effectively cooperate in missionary work in his or her daily life, through prayer, witness and works.

§ 2. Evangelization takes place especially by the proclamation of divine mercy, in a variety of forms and expressions. In a particular way, the specific activity of the Missionaries of Mercy contributes to this end; the Section promotes and supports their training and provides criteria for their pastoral activity.

Art. 60

§ 1. In the context of evangelization, the Section affirms and promotes religious freedom in all social and political settings, in the real situations of the world. In this regard, the Section also avails itself of the cooperation of the Secretariat of State.

§ 2. As an approach to evangelization, the Section encourages and supports, in cooperation with the Dicastery for Interreligious Dialogue and the Dicastery for Culture and

Education, and in accordance with their specific competencies, opportunities for encounter and dialogue with members of other religions and those of no religion.

Section for the First Evangelization and New Particular Churches

Art. 61

This Section supports the proclamation of the Gospel and the deepening of the life of faith in territories of first evangelization and is responsible for all that concerns the erection or modification of ecclesiastical circumscriptions, their provision and carries out other tasks, analogous to those carried out by the Dicastery for Bishops in the area of its own competence.

Art. 62

The Section, in accordance with the principle of just autonomy, supports new particular Churches in the work of initial evangelization and in their growth, in cooperation with the particular Churches, Episcopal Conferences, Institutes of Consecrated Life and Societies of Apostolic Life, associations, ecclesial movements, new communities and ecclesial welfare agencies.

Art. 63

The Section cooperates with Bishops, Episcopal Conferences and Institutes of Consecrated Life and Societies of Apostolic Life in fostering missionary vocations on the part of clerics, members of Institutes of Consecrated Life and Societies of Apostolic Life and laity, as well as in training the secular clergy and catechists in the territories subject to the Dicastery, without prejudice to the competencies of other

Dicasteries in specific areas such as: the academic training of clerics, institutes of higher education, formation and culture.

Art. 64

§ 1. The Section promotes the exchange of experiences within new particular Churches and between them and Churches of older date.

§ 2. It assists the integration of new particular Churches and encourages other Churches to offer them solidary and fraternal support.

§ 3. It provides and organizes courses of initial and continuing formation for Bishops and those equivalent to them, within the territories of its competence.

Art. 65

To increase missionary cooperation, the Section:

1. seeks to help new particular Churches to become financially independent by working with them to create the necessary conditions for this;

2. helps to establish the funds needed to support new particular Churches and to prepare competent personnel for collecting those funds and for cooperating with other particular Churches;

3. promotes among new particular Churches and their groupings the creation of agencies of administration and oversight for the effective use of resources and the quality of investments;

4. supports new particular Churches in the management of personnel.

Art. 66

The Section handles everything having to do with the quinquennial reports and the visits *ad limina Apostolorum* of the particular Churches entrusted to its care.

Art. 67

§ 1. The Section for the First Evangelization and New Particular Churches is entrusted with Pontifical Mission Societies: the Society for the Propagation of the Faith, the Society of Saint Peter the Apostle, the Holy Childhood Association and the Pontifical Missionary Union of Priests and Religious, as instruments for promoting responsibility for the missions on the part of all the baptized and for the support of new particular Churches.

§ 2. The management of the economic subsidies designated for missionary work and their equitable distribution are entrusted to the Adjunct Secretary of the Section who holds the position of President of the Pontifical Mission Societies.

Art. 68

The patrimony set aside for the missions is administered through its own special office, headed by the Adjunct Secretary of the Section, without prejudice to the obligation to render due account to the Secretariat for the Economy.

Dicastery for the Doctrine of the Faith

Art. 69

The task of the Dicastery for the Doctrine of the Faith is to help the Roman Pontiff and the Bishops to proclaim the Gospel throughout the world by promoting and safeguarding the integrity of Catholic teaching on faith and morals. It does this by drawing upon the deposit of faith and seeking an ever deeper understanding of it in the face of new questions.

Art. 70

The Dicastery consists of two Sections: Doctrinal and Disciplinary, each coordinated by a Secretary who assists the Prefect in accordance with the specific area of its competence.

Art. 71

The Doctrinal Section encourages and supports study and reflection on the understanding of faith and morals and the progress of theology in different cultures in the light of sound doctrine and contemporary challenges, in order to offer a response, in light of the faith, to the questions and arguments arising from scientific advances and cultural developments.

Art. 72

§ 1. On the measures to be taken for safeguarding faith and morals and protecting their integrity from errors disseminated by whatever means, the Doctrinal Section carries out its work in close contact with diocesan/eparchial Bishops – whether individually or assembled in Episcopal Conferences, particular Councils or in the hierarchical structures of the Eastern Churches – in the exercise of their mission as authentic teachers and doctors of the faith, whereby they are obliged to preserve and promote the integrity of that faith.

§ 2. This cooperation applies especially in the case of authorization for the teaching of the theological disciplines, for which the Section offers its considered opinion, with due respect for the proper competence of the Dicastery for Culture and Education.

Art. 73

For safeguarding the truth of the faith and the integrity of morals, the Doctrinal Section:

1. examines writings and opinions that appear contrary or harmful to right faith and morals; it seeks a dialogue with the authors of these works and presents suitable remedies to be applied, in accordance with its proper norms;

2. works to ensure that errors and dangerous teachings circulating among the Christian people do not go without suitable rebuttal.

Art. 74

The Doctrinal Section, through its marriage office, is to examine, both in law and in fact, all matters concerning the *privilegium fidei*.

Art. 75

Documents to be published by other Dicasteries, Institutions or Offices of the Roman Curia, insofar as they concern teaching on faith and morals, are to be subjected beforehand to the considered judgment of the Doctrinal Section, which through a process of discussion and mutual understanding will help in making appropriate decisions.

Art. 76

§ 1. The Disciplinary Section, through its disciplinary office, deals with delicts reserved to the Dicastery and adjudicated by the Supreme Apostolic Tribunal established therein, which then declares or imposes canonical sanctions according to the norm of law, both common and proper, without prejudice to the competence of the Apostolic Penitentiary.

§ 2. With regard to the delicts mentioned in § 1, the Section, by mandate of the Roman Pontiff, will judge Cardinals, Patriarchs, Legates of the Apostolic See and Bishops, as well as other physical persons, in conformity with canonical provisions.

§ 3. The Section promotes the training programmes offered by the Dicastery to Ordinaries and legal professionals in order to foster a proper understanding and application of the canonical norms related to its proper area of competency.

Art. 77
Established within the Dicastery are the Pontifical Biblical Commission and the International Theological Commission, both of which are headed by the Prefect. Each operates according to its own approved norms.

Art. 78
§ 1. Established within the Dicastery is the Pontifical Commission for the Protection of Minors, charged with providing guidance and advice to the Roman Pontiff, as well as proposing the most appropriate measures for safeguarding minors and vulnerable persons.

§ 2. The Pontifical Commission assists diocesan/eparchial Bishops, Episcopal Conferences and the hierarchical structures of the Eastern Churches, and the Superiors of Institutes of Consecrated Life and Societies of Apostolic Life and their Conferences, in developing guidelines that propose suitable strategies and procedures for protecting minors and vulnerable persons from sexual abuse and provide an appropriate response to such conduct on the part of the clergy and members of Institutes of Consecrated Life and Societies of

Apostolic Life, in accordance with canonical norms and in due consideration of the requirements of civil law.

§ 3. The members of the Pontifical Commission are appointed by the Roman Pontiff for a term of five years and are chosen from among clerics, members of Institutes of Consecrated Life and Societies of Apostolic Life and lay men and women of various nations who are distinguished for their expertise, proven ability and pastoral experience.

§ 4. The Pontifical Commission is presided by a President Delegate and a Secretary, both of whom are appointed by the Roman Pontiff for a term of five years.

§ 5. The Pontifical Commission has its own officials and carries out its work in accordance with its own approved norms.

Dicastery for the Service of Charity

Art. 79
The Dicastery for the Service of Charity, also known as the Office of the Papal Almoner, is a special expression of mercy and, based on the option for the poor, vulnerable and excluded, carries out in every part of the world the work of aid and assistance offered in the name of the Roman Pontiff, who in cases of particular need or other emergencies, personally determines the forms of aid to be given.

Art. 80
The Dicastery, under the guidance of the Prefect, the Almoner of His Holiness, in contact with the other competent Dicasteries, demonstrates, by its activity, the solicitude and closeness of the Roman Pontiff, as Pastor of the universal

Church, toward those experiencing situations of extreme need, exclusion and poverty, as well as grave disasters.

Art. 81

§ 1. The Dicastery is competent to receive, seek and request voluntary donations for the works of charity that the Roman Pontiff carries out for those most in need.

§ 2. The Almoner of His Holiness also has the faculty to grant the Apostolic Blessing through properly authenticated parchments.

Dicastery for the Eastern Churches

Art. 82

§ 1. The Dicastery deals with those matters involving persons or things, that affect the Eastern Catholic Churches *sui iuris*.

§ 2. Since some of these Churches, especially the ancient patriarchal Churches, are of ancient tradition, the Dicastery will examine on a case-by-case basis, after having consulted, if necessary, other Dicasteries involved, questions that deal with matters related to internal governance that can be left to the higher authorities of those Churches, derogating from the Code of Canons of the Eastern Churches.

Art. 83

§ 1. The Patriarchs and Major Archbishops of Eastern Churches *sui iuris*, and the Prefect of the Dicastery for Promoting Christian Unity, are members of the Dicastery by law.

§ 2. To the extent possible, its consultors and officials are to be chosen from both Eastern rite faithful of the various Churches *sui iuris* and from Latin rite faithful.

Art. 84

§ 1. The Dicastery is competent in all matters pertaining to the Eastern Churches that must be referred to the Apostolic See regarding the structure and organization of those Churches; the exercise of the functions of teaching, sanctifying and governing; and the status, rights, and obligations of persons. It also handles the procedures involving quinquennial reports and visits *ad limina Apostolorum*.

§ 2. With regard to § 1, the proper and exclusive competence of the Dicasteries for the Doctrine of the Faith, the Causes of Saints, and Legislative Texts, as well as that of the Apostolic Penitentiary, the Supreme Tribunal of the Apostolic Signatura and the Tribunal of the Roman Rota, always remains intact.

§ 3. In matters that also affect the faithful of the Latin Church, before proceeding, the Dicastery will consult, if the importance of the matter requires it, the Dicastery competent in the same matters for the faithful of the Latin Church.

Art. 85

The Dicastery pays close attention to communities of Eastern faithful living within the circumscriptions of the Latin Church, and attends to their spiritual needs by providing visitators and, insofar as is possible, a proper hierarchy in cases where numbers and circumstances demand it, following consultation with the Dicastery competent for the establishment of particular Churches in that territory.

Art. 86

In regions where Eastern rites have been more numerous from ancient times, the apostolate and missionary activity depend solely on this Dicastery, even if they are carried out by missionaries belonging to the Latin Church.

Art. 87

The Dicastery carries out its work in cooperation with the Dicastery for Promoting Christian Unity in those matters involving relations with non-Catholic Eastern Churches and with the Dicastery for Interreligious Dialogue and the Dicastery for Culture and Education in matters that concern these.

Dicastery for Divine Worship and the Discipline of the Sacraments

Art. 88

The Dicastery for Divine Worship and the Discipline of the Sacraments promotes the sacred liturgy in accordance with the renewal undertaken by the Second Vatican Council. Its areas of competence include all matters that pertain by law to the Apostolic See concerning the regulation and promotion of the sacred liturgy and vigilance in ensuring that the laws of the Church and the liturgical norms are faithfully observed in every place.

Art. 89

§ 1. It is the task of the Dicastery to provide for the redaction or the revision and updating of the typical editions of liturgical books.

§ 2. The Dicastery confirms the translations of liturgical books in current languages and grants the *recognitio* to the fitting adaptations of these to local cultures, as legitimately approved by the Episcopal Conferences. It also grants the *recognitio* to particular calendars and to the Propers of Masses and the Liturgy of the Hours of particular Churches and Institutes of Consecrated Life and Societies of Apostolic Life, following their approval by the relative competent authority.

§ 3. The Dicastery assists diocesan Bishops and Episcopal Conferences in promoting, by effective and suitable measures, the liturgical apostolate, especially with regard to the celebration of the Eucharist, the other sacraments and liturgical acts, for the sake of an ever more active participation on the part of the faithful. With the Episcopal Conferences, the Dicastery encourages reflection on possible forms of inculturation of the liturgy and accompanies their contextualization.

Art. 90

§ 1. The Dicastery oversees the discipline of the sacraments and juridical issues involving their valid and licit celebration, as well as the discipline of sacramentals, without prejudice to the competence of the Dicastery for the Doctrine of the Faith.

§ 2. It examines and grants requests for indults and dispensations concerning matters that exceed the competencies of diocesan Bishops.

Art. 91

The Dicastery promotes and organizes the periodic celebration of International Eucharistic Congresses and is available to cooperate in the celebration of National Eucharistic Congresses.

Art. 92

The Dicastery is responsible for matters concerning liturgical life:

1. by promoting liturgical formation at various levels, also through multi-regional meetings;

2. by supporting commissions or institutes created for promoting the liturgical apostolate, music, chant and sacred art;

3. by erecting international associations for these purposes or by approving their statutes.

Art. 93

The Dicastery is responsible for the regulation and discipline of the sacred liturgy with regard to the use – permitted according to the established norms – of liturgical books in use prior to the reform of the Second Vatican Council.

Art. 94

The Dicastery is responsible for preserving the veneration of sacred relics, the confirmation of patron saints and the granting of the title of minor basilica.

Art. 95

The Dicastery assists diocesan Bishops in ensuring that the forms of popular devotion increasingly conform to the Church's norms and are in harmony with the sacred liturgy, by affirming its principles and providing guidance for their fruitful implementation in the particular Churches.

Art. 96

The Dicastery assists Bishops in carrying out their proper office as moderators, promoters and guardians of the entire liturgical life of the particular Church entrusted to their care, by offering guidelines and suggestions for promoting a correct liturgical formation, in order to prevent and eliminate possible abuses.

Art. 97

To carry out its responsibilities more effectively, the Dicastery can, in addition to its members and consultors, seek cooperation and periodic exchanges with the liturgical commissions of the various Episcopal Conferences and with the international committees for the translation of liturgical books into the major languages; it also follows with interest the contributions made in the area of liturgy by institutions of higher ecclesiastical studies.

Dicastery for the Causes of Saints

Art. 98

The Dicastery for the Causes of Saints, in accordance with its prescribed procedure, treats all that pertains to causes of beatification and canonization.

Art. 99

§ 1. The Dicastery provides special norms and assists with advice and direction the diocesan/eparchial Bishops who are responsible for the instruction of a cause.

§ 2. It examines the acts of causes already instructed, verifying that the process was carried out properly and expressing a judgment on the merits of those causes, in order to submit them to the Roman Pontiff.

Art. 100

The Dicastery oversees the application of the norms regulating the administration of the fund established to cover the expenses of causes.

Art. 101

The Dicastery determines the canonical procedure for verifying and declaring the authenticity of sacred relics and for ensuring their preservation.

Art. 102

The Dicastery is also competent to make a determination regarding the granting of the title *Doctor of the Church* to a given saint, after having received the *votum* of the Dicastery for the Doctrine of the Faith concerning his or her outstanding teaching.

Dicastery for Bishops

Art. 103

The Dicastery for Bishops is responsible for all matters pertaining to the establishment and provision of particular Churches and to the exercise of the episcopal office in the Latin Church, without prejudice to the competence of the Dicastery for Evangelization.

Art. 104

The Dicastery, after collecting the necessary information and in cooperation with the Bishops and Episcopal Conferences, deals with all matters concerning the constitution, division, union, suppression, and any other changes of particular Churches and of their groupings. It is also responsible for erecting military Ordinariates as well as personal Ordinariates for the Anglican faithful who enter into full communion with the Catholic Church within the territory of a given Episcopal Conference, after having consulted the Dicastery for the Doctrine of the Faith and the Conference involved.

Art. 105

§ 1. The Dicastery deals with all matters concerning the appointment of diocesan and titular Bishops, Apostolic Administrators and, in general, the provision of the particular Churches. It does so by considering the proposals presented by the particular Churches, the Episcopal Conferences and the Papal Representations, and after having consulted the executive officers of the respective Episcopal Conference and the Metropolitan. In appropriate ways, it also engages in this process the members of the people of God of the dioceses in question.

§ 2. The Dicastery, in consultation with the Episcopal Conferences and their regional and continental groupings, determines the criteria for the selection of candidates. These criteria must take into account differing cultural needs and are to be periodically evaluated.

§ 3. The Dicastery also deals with the resignation of Bishops from their office, in conformity with the canonical norms.

Art. 106

Whenever discussions with civil governments are required, either for the establishment or modification of particular Churches and their groupings or the provision of those Churches, the Dicastery will proceed only after consultation with the Section for Relations with States and International

Organizations of the Secretariat of State and the Episcopal Conferences involved.

Art. 107

§ 1. The Dicastery readily cooperates with the Bishops in all matters concerning the correct and fruitful exercise of the pastoral office entrusted to them.

§ 2. In cases where the correct exercise of the episcopal function of governance calls for a special intervention, and the Metropolitan or the Episcopal Conferences are not able to resolve the problem, it falls to the Dicastery, if necessary in accord with other competent Dicasteries, to decide upon fraternal or apostolic visitations and, proceeding in like manner, to evaluate their outcome and to propose to the Roman Pontiff the measures deemed appropriate.

Art. 108

The Dicastery handles everything dealing with the *ad limina Apostolorum* visits of the particular Churches assigned to its care. To this end, it studies the reports submitted by the Bishops in accordance with art. 40; it assists the Bishops during their stay in Rome, arranging their meeting with the Roman Pontiff, their pilgrimages to the Papal Basilicas and other meetings. When the visit is completed, the Dicastery communicates in writing its conclusions, suggestions and proposals for the respective particular Churches and Episcopal Conferences.

Art. 109

§ 1. The Dicastery, without prejudice to the competence of the Dicastery for Evangelization, is responsible for the formation of new Bishops, with the help of Bishops of proven wisdom, prudence and experience, as well as experts from various parts of the universal Church.

§ 2. The Dicastery periodically offers to the Bishops occasions for permanent formation and courses of continuing education.

Art. 110

The Dicastery carries out its work in a spirit of service and in close cooperation with the Episcopal Conferences and their regional and continental groupings. It seeks to do likewise with regard to the celebration of particular Councils, the establishment of Episcopal Conferences and the *recognitio* of their statutes. The Dicastery receives the acts and decrees of the above-mentioned bodies. It examines them in consultation with the other Dicasteries involved, and grants the required *recognitio* to the decrees. It also carries out everything prescribed by the canonical norms concerning ecclesiastical provinces and regions.

Art. 111

§ 1. Established within the Dicastery is the Pontifical Commission for Latin America, which is responsible for studying questions regarding the life and growth of those particular Churches as a means of assisting the Dicasteries that deal with them by reason of their competence, and to help those Churches with advice and economic resources.

§ 2. It is also responsible for fostering relations between international and national ecclesiastical institutions working in the regions of Latin America and with the institutions of the Curia.

Art. 112

§ 1. The President of the Commission is the Prefect of the Dicastery for Bishops, assisted by one or more Secretaries. They have as counsellors Bishops chosen from both the Roman Curia and the Churches of Latin America. The Secretary and the counsellors are appointed by the Roman Pontiff for a term of five years.

§ 2. The members of the Commission are chosen from the institutions of the Curia, the Latin American Episcopal Council (CELAM), Bishops from the regions of Latin America, and the institutions mentioned in the preceding article. They are appointed by the Roman Pontiff for a term of five years.

§ 3. The Commission has its own officials.

Dicastery for the Clergy

Art. 113

§ 1. The Dicastery for the Clergy deals with all matters relating to priests and deacons of the diocesan clergy, with regard to their persons and pastoral ministry, and everything needed for the fruitful exercise of the latter. In these matters, it provides suitable assistance to the Bishops.

§ 2. The Dicastery expresses and implements the solicitude of the Apostolic See with regard to the training of candidates for Holy Orders.

Art. 114

§ 1. The Dicastery assists diocesan Bishops in promoting vocations to the ordained ministry in their Churches and in ensuring that, in seminaries established and conducted in accordance with the law, students are suitably trained and receive a solid human, spiritual, intellectual and pastoral formation.

§ 2. For those matters that by law are the competence of the Holy See, the Dicastery ensures that community life and the governance of seminaries conform to the requirements of seminary formation and that the Superiors and educators make every effort to contribute by their example and sound doctrine to forming the character of future ordained ministers.

§ 3. The Dicastery is responsible for promoting all that concerns the training of future clerics by issuing appropriate norms, such as the *Ratio Fundamentalis Institutionis Sacerdotalis* and the *Ratio Fundamentalis Institutionis Diaconorum Permanentium*, as well as other documents regarding ongoing formation.

§ 4. The Dicastery is competent to confirm the *Ratio Institutionis Sacerdotalis Nationalis* issued by the various Episcopal Conferences, and to confirm the erection of inter-diocesan seminaries and their statutes.

§ 5. In order to ensure and improve the quality of priestly formation, the Dicastery promotes the establishment of inter-diocesan seminaries in places where diocesan seminaries cannot offer an adequate formation with a sufficient number of candidates, properly qualified formators, instructors and spiritual directors, as well as other structures necessary for supporting them.

Art. 115

§ 1. The Dicastery offers assistance to diocesan Bishops and Episcopal Conferences in their respective activities of gov-

ernance with regard to the life, discipline, rights and obligations of clerics, and it cooperates with them concerning the
permanent formation of clerics. It ensures, furthermore, that
diocesan Bishops or Episcopal Conferences provide for the
sustenance and social welfare of the clergy in accordance
with the law.

§ 2. It is competent to examine through an administrative
process the disputes and hierarchical recourses presented
by clerics, including members of Institutes of Consecrated
Life and Societies of Apostolic Life, where the exercise of the
ministry is concerned, without prejudice to the prescriptions
of art. 28 § 1.

§ 3. It studies, with the help of the competent Dicasteries,
problems resulting from the shortage of priests in various
parts of the world, which on the one hand deprives the
people of God from the possibility of participating in the
Eucharist and on the other weakens the sacramental structure of the Church. It therefore encourages Bishops and
Episcopal Conferences to provide for a more adequate distribution of clergy.

Art. 116
§ 1. The Dicastery is responsible for handling, in conformity
with the canonical norms, matters having to do with the
clerical state as such, for all clergy, including members of
Institutes of Consecrated Life and Societies of Apostolic
Life, and for permanent deacons, in cooperation with the
competent Dicasteries whenever circumstances so demand.

§ 2. The Dicastery is competent for cases of dispensation
from the obligations assumed by ordination to the diaconate

and priesthood involving diocesan clerics and members of Institutes of Consecrated Life and Societies of Apostolic Life from the Latin Church and from the Eastern Churches.

Art. 117
The Dicastery has competence for all matters that pertain to the Holy See with regard to Personal Prelatures.

Art. 118
The Dicastery deals with those matters in which the Holy See is competent regarding:

1. the general discipline governing diocesan finance councils, presbyteral councils, colleges of consultors, chapters of canons, diocesan pastoral councils, parishes and churches;

2. associations of clerics and public clerical associations; to the latter it can grant the faculty to incardinate, after having consulted the competent Dicasteries and having received the approval of the Roman Pontiff;

3. ecclesiastical archives;

4. the extinction of pious wills in general and of pious foundations.

Art. 119
The Dicastery carries out everything that pertains to the Holy See regarding the regulation of ecclesiastical goods, especially their correct management, and it grants the necessary permissions and approvals, without prejudice to the Dicasteries for Evangelization, the Eastern Churches and Institutes of Consecrated Life and Societies of Apostolic Life.

Art. 120

Established within the Dicastery are the Pontifical Work for Priestly Vocations and the Permanent Interdicasteral Commission for the formation for Holy Orders, presided over *ex officio* by the Prefect.

Dicastery for Institutes of Consecrated Life and Societies of Apostolic Life

Art. 121

The competence of the Dicastery is to promote, encourage and regulate the practice of the evangelical counsels, how they are lived out in the approved forms of consecrated life and all matters concerning the life and activity of Societies of Apostolic Life throughout the Latin Church.

Art. 122

§ 1. It pertains to the Dicastery to approve the Institutes of Consecrated Life and Societies of Apostolic Life, to erect them and also to grant permission for the validity of the establishment of an Institute of Consecrated Life or Society of Apostolic Life of diocesan right on the part of the Bishop.

§ 2. Mergers, unions and suppressions of Institutes of Consecrated Life and Societies of Apostolic Life are also reserved to the Dicastery.

§ 3. The Dicastery is competent for approving and regulating forms of consecrated life that are new with respect to those already recognized by law.

§ 4. It is the task of the Dicastery to erect or suppress unions, confederations, and federations of Institutes of Consecrated Life and Societies of Apostolic Life.

Art. 123

The Dicastery works to ensure that Institutes of Consecrated Life and Societies of Apostolic Life make progress in following Christ in conformity with the Gospel according to their proper charism stemming from the spirit of the founder and sound traditions, that they faithfully pursue their own ends and contribute effectively to the building up of the Church and to its mission in the world.

Art. 124

§ 1. In accordance with canonical norms, the Dicastery deals with matters belonging to the competence of the Apostolic See regarding the life and activity of the Institutes of Consecrated Life and Societies of Apostolic Life, particularly with regard to:

1. the approval of Constitutions and their amendments;

2. ordinary government and discipline of members;

3. the incorporation and formation of members, including through specific norms and directives;

4. temporal goods and their administration;

5. the apostolate;

6. extraordinary measures of governance.

§ 2. The following also belong to the competence of the Dicastery, according to the norm of law:

1. the transfer of a member to another approved form of consecrated life;

2. the extension of absence and exclaustration beyond the term granted by the supreme Moderators;

3. the indult for members in perpetual vows to depart from Institutes of Consecrated Life or Societies of Apostolic Life of Pontifical right;

4. imposed exclaustration;

5. the examination of appeals against the decree of dismissal of members.

Art. 125
It is the competence of the Dicastery to erect international Conferences of Major Superiors, to approve their statutes and to ensure that their activities are ordered to their proper ends.

Art. 126
§ 1. The eremitical life and the *Ordo Virginum* are subject to the Dicastery inasmuch as they are forms of consecrated life.

§ 2. It is the Dicastery's task to establish associations of the *Ordo Virginum* at the international level.

Art. 127
The competence of the Dicastery also extends to Third Orders and associations of the faithful erected with a view to becoming an Institute of Consecrated Life or a Society of Apostolic Life.

Dicastery for the Laity, the Family and Life

Art. 128
§ 1. The Dicastery for the Laity, the Family and Life is competent for enhancing the apostolate of the lay faithful, the pastoral care of young people, the family and its mission

according to God's plan, the elderly, and for the promotion and protection of life.

§ 2. In carrying out its responsibilities, the Dicastery maintains relationships with the particular Churches, with Episcopal Conferences, their regional and continental groupings, the hierarchical structures of the Eastern Churches and other ecclesial entities, promoting exchanges between them and offering its cooperation so that the values and initiatives connected to these matters may be promoted.

Art. 129
In enlivening and encouraging the promotion of the vocation and mission of the lay faithful in the Church and in the world, the Dicastery cooperates with the various lay ecclesial organizations so that the lay faithful share both their experiences of faith in diverse social contexts and their own secular skills in the Church's pastoral ministry and governance.

Art. 130
The Dicastery expresses the Church's special concern for young people, promoting their leading role amid the world's challenges. It supports the Roman Pontiff's initiatives in the field of youth ministry and places itself at the service of Episcopal Conferences, of the hierarchical structures of the Eastern Churches, and of international youth movements and associations, fostering their cooperation and organizing meetings on the international level.

Art. 131
The Dicastery seeks to deepen reflection on the relationship between men and women in their respective specificity,

reciprocity, complementarity and equal dignity. It offers its own contribution to ecclesial reflection on the identity and mission of women and men in the Church and in society by promoting their participation, appreciating the distinctive characteristics of women and men, and developing role models for women in the Church.

Art. 132
The Dicastery studies issues relating to cooperation between the laity and ordained ministers in virtue of their baptism and the diversity of charisms and ministries, in order to foster in both an awareness of co-responsibility for the life and mission of the Church.

Art. 133
It is the competence of the Dicastery, with the agreement of other Dicasteries concerned, to evaluate and approve the proposals of Episcopal Conferences relating to the institution of new ministries and ecclesiastical offices to be entrusted to the laity, according to the needs of the particular Churches.

Art. 134
Within the sphere of its own competence, the Dicastery accompanies the life and development of groups of the faithful and of ecclesial movements, recognizing or erecting, in conformity with the provisions of canon law, those which have an international character and approving their statutes, without prejudice to the competence of the Secretariat of State. It also deals with possible hierarchical appeals relating to the common life and apostolate of the laity.

Art. 135

The Dicastery promotes the pastoral care of marriage and the family on the basis of the teachings of the Church's magisterium. It works to ensure the recognition of the rights and duties of spouses and of families in the Church, society and in economic and political life. It promotes international meetings and events.

Art. 136

In coordination with the Dicasteries for Evangelization and for Culture and Education, the Dicastery supports the development and sharing of models for transmitting the faith within families and encourages parents to practice their faith in daily life. It also promotes inclusive models in pastoral care and education.

Art. 137

§ 1. The Dicastery examines, with the input of Episcopal Conferences and the hierarchical structures of the Eastern Churches, the variety of anthropological, socio-cultural and economic conditions of the lives of married couples and families.

§ 2. With the help of experts, the Dicastery studies and analyses the major causes of crises within marriages and families, paying particular attention to the experiences of those involved in marital breakdowns, especially children, in order to encourage greater awareness of the value of the family and the role of parents in society and in the Church.

§ 3. It is the task of the Dicastery, in cooperation with Episcopal Conferences and the hierarchical structures of the Eastern Churches, to collect and propose models of pastoral accompaniment, of formation of consciences and of integration for the divorced and civilly remarried and also for those in certain cultures who live in situations of polygamy.

Art. 138

§ 1. The Dicastery supports initiatives in favour of responsible procreation, as well as for the protection of human life from conception to its natural end, bearing in mind the needs of the person in the various stages of development.

§ 2. The Dicastery promotes and encourages organizations and associations that help families and individuals to welcome and responsibly safeguard the gift of life, especially in the case of difficult pregnancies, and prevent recourse to abortion. It also supports programmes and initiatives of particular Churches, Episcopal Conferences and hierarchical structures of the Eastern Churches aimed at helping those involved in an abortion.

Art. 139

§ 1. The Dicastery studies the main issues in biomedicine and law relating to human life, in dialogue with the various theological disciplines and other relevant sciences, based on the Church's magisterium. It examines developing theories about human life and the reality of humanity. In studying the aforementioned questions, the Dicastery proceeds in consultation with the Dicastery for the Doctrine of the Faith.

§ 2. In the same way, it reflects on changes in social life, in order to promote the full and harmonious development of human persons, valuing progress and taking stock of trends that hinder this development on the cultural and social level.

Art. 140

The Dicastery follows the activities of Catholic institutions, associations, movements and organizations, both nationally and internationally, whose purpose is to serve the good of the family.

Art. 141

§ 1. The Dicastery cooperates with the Pontifical Academy for Life, and avails itself of its competence, on issues concerning the protection and promotion of human life.

§ 2. The Dicastery works with the Pontifical John Paul II Theological Institute for Matrimonial and Family Science, both with the central session and with the other sessions and associated/linked centres, in order to promote a common direction for studies on marriage, family and life.

Dicastery for Promoting Christian Unity

Art. 142

It belongs to the Dicastery for Promoting Christian Unity to engage in timely ecumenical initiatives and activities, both within the Catholic Church and in relations with other Churches and Ecclesial Communities, in order to restore unity among Christians.

Art. 143

§ 1. It is the task of the Dicastery to implement the teachings of the Second Vatican Council and of the post-conciliar magisterium on ecumenism.

§ 2. It deals with the correct interpretation and faithful application of ecumenical principles and established directives in order to guide, coordinate and develop ecumenical activity.

§ 3. It promotes Catholic meetings and events, both nationally and internationally, suitable for promoting Christian unity.

§ 4. The Dicastery coordinates the ecumenical initiatives of other curial institutions, offices and institutions associated with the Holy See with other Churches and Ecclesial Communities.

Art. 144

§ 1. Having previously submitted matters to the Roman Pontiff, the Dicastery takes care of relations with other Churches and Ecclesial Communities. It promotes theological dialogue and meetings in order to foster unity with them, making use of the cooperation of experts.

§ 2. The Dicastery appoints the Catholic members of theological dialogues, and the Catholic observers and delegates for the various ecumenical meetings. Whenever it seems appropriate, it invites observers, or fraternal delegates of other Churches and Ecclesial Communities to the most significant meetings and events of the Catholic Church.

§ 3. The Dicastery fosters ecumenical initiatives also on the spiritual, pastoral and cultural levels.

Art. 145

§ 1. Since the Dicastery, by its very nature, must often deal with questions pertaining to the faith, it is necessary that it proceed in consultation with the Dicastery for the Doctrine of the Faith, especially when it comes to issuing public documents or declarations.

§ 2. In dealing with matters concerning relations between the Eastern Catholic Churches and the Orthodox or Oriental

Orthodox Churches, it cooperates with the Dicastery for the Eastern Churches and the Secretariat of State.

Art. 146

In order to advance the relationship between Catholics and Jews, the Commission for Religious Relations with the Jews is established within the Dicastery. The Commission is directed by the Prefect.

Dicastery for Interreligious Dialogue

Art. 147

The Dicastery for Interreligious Dialogue promotes and supervises relations with members and groups of non-Christian religions, with the exception of Judaism, competence for which belongs to the Dicastery for Promoting Christian Unity.

Art. 148

The Dicastery works to ensure that dialogue with the followers of other religions takes place in an appropriate way, with an attitude of listening, esteem and respect. It fosters various kinds of relations with them so that, through the contribution of all, peace, freedom, social justice, the protection and safeguarding of creation, and spiritual and moral values may be promoted.

Art. 149

§ 1. Aware that interreligious dialogue takes place through action, theological exchange and spiritual experience, the Dicastery encourages a true search for God among all people. It promotes timely studies and conferences in order to enhance mutual knowledge and esteem, so that human dignity and the spiritual and moral riches of people can grow.

§ 2. It is the Dicastery's task to assist diocesan/eparchial Bishops in the formation of those who engage in interreligious dialogue.

Art. 150
§ 1. Recognizing the different religious traditions that sincerely seek God, the Dicastery provides specialized personnel for these different areas.

§ 2. In order to promote relations with followers of different religious beliefs, Commissions are established in the Dicastery under the direction of the Prefect and in cooperation with the relevant Episcopal Conferences and hierarchical structures of the Eastern Churches, including the Commission for Religious Relations with Muslims.

Art. 151
In the exercise of its functions, the Dicastery, when required, proceeds in consultation with the Dicastery for the Doctrine of the Faith and, if necessary, with the Dicasteries for the Eastern Churches and for Evangelization.

Art. 152
§ 1. In carrying out its functions, the Dicastery proceeds and plans its initiatives in consultation with the particular Churches, Episcopal Conferences, their regional and continental groupings and the hierarchical structures of the Eastern Churches.

§ 2. The Dicastery also encourages particular Churches to undertake initiatives in the field of interreligious dialogue.

Dicastery for Culture and Education

Art. 153

§ 1. The Dicastery for Culture and Education works for the development of people's human values in the context of Christian anthropology, contributing to the full realization of Christian discipleship.

§ 2. The Dicastery comprises the Section for Culture, dedicated to the promotion of culture, pastoral activity and the enhancement of cultural heritage, and the Section for Education, which develops the fundamental principles of education regarding schools, Catholic and ecclesiastical institutes of higher education and research, and is competent for hierarchical recourses in these matters.

Art. 154

The Section for Culture promotes and supports relations between the Holy See and the world of culture. It responds to the many issues therein with a preference for dialogue as an indispensable tool of true encounter, mutual interaction and enrichment, in order that different cultures may become ever more open to the Gospel, as likewise the Christian faith towards them, and that lovers of the arts, literature, the sciences, technology and sport may know and feel recognized by the Church as people at the service of a sincere search for the true, the good and the beautiful.

Art. 155

The Section for Culture offers its assistance and cooperation so that diocesan/eparchial Bishops, Episcopal Conferences and the hierarchical structures of the Eastern Churches may protect and preserve their historical patrimony, particularly documents and juridical instruments concerning and attesting to the life and pastoral care of ecclesial entities, as well as their artistic and cultural heritage. These should be kept with the utmost care in archives, libraries and museums, churches and other buildings in order that they be available to all interested parties.

Art. 156

§ 1. The Section for Culture promotes and encourages dialogue between the diverse cultures present within the Church, thus fostering mutual enrichment.

§ 2. It seeks to ensure that diocesan/eparchial Bishops, Episcopal Conferences and the hierarchical structures of the Eastern Churches enhance and protect local cultures with their patrimony of wisdom and spirituality as a resource for the whole human family.

Art. 157

§ 1. The Section for Culture arranges appropriate initiatives concerning culture; it follows projects undertaken by particular institutions of the Church and, where necessary, offers them its cooperation, without prejudice to the autonomy of their respective research programmes.

§ 2. In consultation with the Secretariat of State, it shows an interest in and follows the action programmes undertaken by States and international institutions aimed at the promotion of culture and the enhancement of cultural patrimony. It participates in these areas, as opportunity allows, in international forums and specialized conferences, and it promotes or supports congresses.

Art. 158

The Section for Culture establishes and promotes initiatives of dialogue with those who, though professing no particular religion, sincerely seek an encounter with God's truth. It likewise shows the Church's pastoral concern for those who do not profess any creed.

Art. 159

§ 1. The Section for Education cooperates with diocesan/eparchial Bishops, Episcopal Conferences and the hierarchical structures of the Eastern Churches so that the fundamental principles of education, especially Catholic education, may be welcomed and better understood, enabling them to be implemented contextually and culturally.

§ 2. It supports diocesan/eparchial Bishops, Episcopal Conferences and the hierarchical structures of the Eastern Churches which, in order to promote the Catholic identity of schools and institutes of higher education, can issue norms defining their criteria in a particular cultural context. Together with them, it ensures that the integrity of the Catholic faith is safeguarded in doctrinal teaching.

Art. 160

§ 1. The Section for Education supports diocesan/eparchial Bishops, Episcopal Conferences and the hierarchical structures of the Eastern Churches in establishing the norms according to which Catholic schools of all kinds and levels must be erected, in which provision should also be made for educational pastoral care as part of evangelization.

§ 2. It promotes the teaching of the Catholic faith in schools.

Art. 161

§ 1. The Section for Education cooperates with diocesan/eparchial Bishops, Episcopal Conferences and the hierarchical structures of the Eastern Churches in promoting throughout the whole Church the establishment and development of a sufficient and qualified number of ecclesiastical and Catholic institutes of higher education and of other institutes of study, in which the sacred disciplines and humanistic and scientific studies can be deepened and fostered, taking into account Christian truths. In this way, students can be suitably formed for carrying out their proper roles in the Church and in society.

§ 2. It is competent for fulfilling the necessary requirements in order that academic degrees issued in the name of the Holy See are recognized by States.

§ 3. It is the competent authority for approving and erecting institutes of higher education and other ecclesiastical academic institutions, for approving their statutes and overseeing their observance, in relationship also with civil authorities. As far as Catholic institutes of higher education are concerned, it deals with matters that, by law, fall within the competence of the Holy See.

§ 4. It promotes cooperation between ecclesiastical and Catholic institutes of higher education and their associations.

§ 5. It is responsible for issuing the *nihil obstat* necessary for teachers to be eligible to teach theological disciplines, as foreseen by art. 72 § 2.

§ 6. It cooperates with other competent Dicasteries in supporting diocesan/eparchial Bishops and other Ordinaries and Hierarchs, Episcopal Conferences and the hierarchical structures of the Eastern Churches in the academic formation of clerics, members of Institutes of Consecrated Life and Societies of Apostolic Life and lay people preparing for service in the Church.

Art. 162

The Dicastery for Culture and Education also coordinates the activities of a number of Pontifical Academies, some of long-standing origin, which involve the participation of international figures within the theological and humanistic sciences, chosen from both believers and non-believers. Currently these are: the Pontifical Academy of Fine Arts and Letters of the Virtuosi at the Pantheon; the Pontifical Roman Academy of Archaeology; the Pontifical Academy of Theology; the Pontifical Academy of Saint Thomas Aquinas; the Pontifical International Marian Academy; the Pontifical Academy *Cultorum Martyrum* and the Pontifical Academy for Latin.

Dicastery for Promoting Integral Human Development

Art. 163

§ 1. The Dicastery for Promoting Integral Human Development has the task of promoting the human person and the God-given dignity of all, together with human rights, health, justice and peace. It is principally concerned with matters relating to the economy and work, the care of creation and the earth as our "common home", migration and humanitarian emergencies.

§ 2. It examines and spreads the Church's social doctrine on integral human development and, in the light of the Gospel, recognizes and interprets both the current and future needs and concerns of the human race.

§ 3. It supports the particular Churches, Episcopal Conferences, their regional and continental groupings and the hierarchical structures of the Eastern Churches in the area of integral human promotion, and recognizes their contribution.

§ 4. It makes use of experts from Institutes of Consecrated Life and Societies of Apostolic Life and from organizations for development and humanitarian intervention. It cooperates with the representatives of civil society and international organizations, respecting the competencies of the Secretariat of State.

Art. 164

In cooperation with Episcopal Conferences, their regional and continental groupings and the hierarchical structures of the Eastern Churches, the Dicastery fosters the implementation of the Church's magisterium in the areas of the protection and integral development of the environment, working with members of other Christian confessions and of other religions, with civil authorities and organizations, and with international organizations.

Art. 165

In its activity of promoting justice and peace, the Dicastery:

1. actively works for the prevention and resolution of conflicts, also identifying and analysing their possible causes, in consultation with the Secretariat of State and with the involvement of Episcopal Conferences and the hierarchical structures of the Eastern Churches;

2. undertakes to defend and promote the dignity and fundamental rights of human persons as well as their social, economic and political rights;

3. supports initiatives against human trafficking, forced prostitution, the exploitation of minors and vulnerable individuals and various forms of slavery and torture, and works to ensure that the international community is attentive and sensitive to the issue of the treatment of prisoners and their living conditions and is committed to the abolition of the death penalty;

4. endeavours to ensure that through the particular Churches, effective and appropriate material and spiritual assistance is given – if necessary also through appropriate pastoral structures – to migrants, refugees, displaced persons and others involved in human movement in need of specific pastoral care.

Art. 166

§ 1. Within particular Churches, the Dicastery promotes the pastoral care of seafarers, both at sea and in ports, especially through the Apostolate of the Sea, which it directs.

§ 2. It exercises the same care for those who serve on aircraft or in airports.

Art. 167

The Dicastery, in cooperation with Episcopal Conferences, their regional and continental groupings and the hierarchical structures of the Eastern Churches, promotes the fight against poverty, and works with national and international institutions for the pursuit of integral human development.

It encourages initiatives against corruption and in favour of good governance, so that the public interest may be served and trust in the international community may increase.

Art. 168
The Dicastery promotes and defends equitable economic models and sober lifestyles, especially by promoting initiatives against the economic and social exploitation of poor countries, asymmetrical commercial relations, financial speculation and development models that create exclusion.

Art. 169
The Dicastery cooperates with diocesan/eparchial Bishops, Episcopal Conferences and the hierarchical structures of the Eastern Churches in order to increase awareness of the need for peace, and for the commitment to justice and solidarity towards the weakest and most fragile in society, especially on the occasion of *World Days* dedicated to these themes.

Art. 170
The Dicastery, together with Episcopal Conferences, their regional and continental groupings and the hierarchical structures of the Eastern Churches, analyses – and is committed to overcoming – the main causes of migration and flight from countries of origin. It likewise promotes initiatives of solidarity and integration in the countries of welcome. In consultation with the Secretariat of State, it cooperates with organizations for development and humanitarian interventions and international organizations for the drafting and adoption of norms in favour of refugees, asylum seekers and migrants.

Art. 171

The Dicastery promotes and encourages just and integral health care. It supports the initiatives of Dioceses, Eparchies, Institutes of Consecrated Life, Societies of Apostolic Life, *Caritas* and lay associations in seeking to prevent the marginalization of the sick and disabled, and to overcome the lack of care due to shortages of staff, hospital equipment or the supply of medicines to poor countries. It also devotes attention to the lack of research in the fight against disease.

Art. 172

§ 1. The Dicastery also cooperates with the Secretariat of State in participating in the Holy See's Delegations to intergovernmental meetings on matters pertaining to its competence.

§ 2. On matters regarding relations with civil governments and other subjects of international law, it maintains close relations with the Secretariat of State, especially when it intends to speak publicly through documents or statements.

Art. 173

The Dicastery cooperates with the Holy See's agencies for humanitarian aid in crisis areas, working with ecclesial humanitarian and development organizations.

Art. 174

§ 1. The Dicastery maintains a close relationship with the Pontifical Academy of Social Sciences and the Pontifical Academy for Life, respecting their statutes.

§ 2. It is competent with regard to *Caritas Internationalis* and the International Catholic Migration Commission, according to their statutes.

§ 3. It exercises the responsibilities reserved by law to the Holy See in establishing and supervising international charitable associations and funds created for the same purposes, in accordance with the provisions of the respective statutes and in compliance with current legislation.

Dicastery for Legislative Texts

Art. 175

§ 1. The Dicastery for Legislative Texts promotes and encourages in the Church the understanding and acceptance of the canonical law of the Latin Church and that of the Eastern Churches and offers assistance for its correct application.

§ 2. It performs its duties by serving the Roman Pontiff, the curial institutions and offices, diocesan/eparchial Bishops, Episcopal Conferences, the hierarchical structures of the Eastern Churches, and the Supreme Moderators of Institutes of Consecrated Life and Societies of Apostolic Life of Pontifical right.

§ 3. In the execution of its duties, it cooperates with canonists from different cultures who work in different continents.

Art. 176

It is the function of the Dicastery to formulate the authentic interpretation of the Church's laws, approved *in forma specifica* by the Roman Pontiff as Supreme Legislator and Interpreter, after having consulted, in questions of greater importance, the competent curial institutions and offices of the Roman Curia with regard to the particular matters being considered.

Art. 177

In the event that a doubt about a law arises which does not require an authentic interpretation, the Dicastery can offer appropriate clarifications about the meaning of the norms through an interpretation formulated according to the criteria provided for by canonical legislation. These clarifications can take the form of statements or explanatory notes.

Art. 178

In studying the current legislation of the Latin Church and the Eastern Churches and issues arising from ecclesial practice, the Dicastery examines the possible presence of *lacunae legis* and presents to the Roman Pontiff adequate proposals for overcoming them. It also verifies any need to update current legislation and suggests amendments, ensuring the harmony and effectiveness of the law.

Art. 179

The Dicastery assists curial institutions in preparing general executive decrees, instructions and other texts of a normative character, to ensure that they are in conformity with the prescriptions of current universal law and are drawn up in a correct juridical form.

Art. 180

The general decrees issued by plenary Councils, Episcopal Conferences or the hierarchical structures of the Eastern Churches are submitted to this Dicastery by the Dicastery which is competent to grant them *recognitio*, in order that they be examined from a juridical perspective.

Art. 181

At the request of interested parties, the Dicastery determines whether laws or general decrees issued by legislators below the level of the Roman Pontiff are in conformity with the Church's universal law.

Art. 182

§ 1. The Dicastery fosters the study of the canon law of the Latin Church and of the Eastern Churches and of other legislative texts by organizing interdicasterial meetings, conferences and by promoting international and national associations of canonists.

§ 2. The Dicastery pays particular attention to correct canonical practice, so that law is adequately understood and correctly applied in the Church. When necessary, it likewise alerts the competent authority concerning the emergence of illegitimate practices and offers advice in this regard.

Dicastery for Communication

Art. 183

The Dicastery for Communication oversees the entire communications network of the Apostolic See and, with structural unity and respecting the relative operational characteristics, unifies the Holy See's activities in the area of communication. It does so in order that the whole system responds in an integrated way to the needs of the Church's evangelizing mission in a context characterized by the presence and development of digital media, and by the factors of convergence and interactivity.

Art. 184

The Dicastery meets the needs of the Church's evangelizing mission through the use of production models, technological innovations and forms of communication currently available and those that may yet emerge.

Art. 185

In addition to the operational functions assigned to it, the Dicastery also deepens and develops the properly theological and pastoral aspects of the Church's activity in the field of communication. In this sense, it also works on the level of training, in order that communication not be reduced to purely technological and instrumental concepts.

Art. 186

It pertains to the Dicastery to ensure that the faithful become increasingly aware of their own responsibility to commit themselves to the task of making the multiple means of communication available to the Church's pastoral mission, in service to the growth of civilization and morality. It especially seeks to develop this awareness through the celebration of *World Communications Day*.

Art. 187

In its activities, the Dicastery makes use of the connectivity and network infrastructures of Vatican City State, in accordance with the particular legislation and international commitments undertaken by the Holy See. In fulfilling its functions, it cooperates with the competent curial institutions and in particular with the Secretariat of State.

Art. 188

The Dicastery is to support the communication activities of other curial institutions and offices, institutions associated with the Holy See, the Governorate of Vatican City State, and other entities based in Vatican City State or depending on the Apostolic See.

VI.
INSTITUTIONS OF JUSTICE

Art. 189

§ 1. The service provided by the Institutions of Justice is one of the essential functions in the governance of the Church. The aim of this service, pursued by each institution in the forum of its own competence, is that of the Church's own mission: to proclaim and inaugurate the Kingdom of God and to work, through the order of justice applied with canonical equity, for the salvation of souls, which is always the supreme law in the Church.

§ 2. The ordinary Institutions of Justice are the Apostolic Penitentiary, the Supreme Tribunal of the Apostolic Signatura and the Tribunal of the Roman Rota. The three institutions are independent of each other.

Apostolic Penitentiary

Art. 190

§ 1. The Apostolic Penitentiary is competent in all matters regarding the internal forum and indulgences as expressions of divine mercy.

§ 2. It is headed by the Major Penitentiary, assisted by the Regent and by several officials.

Art. 191

For the internal forum, whether sacramental or non-sacramental, it grants absolution from censures, dispensations, commutations, validations, remissions and other favours.

Art. 192

§ 1. The Apostolic Penitentiary sees to it that the Papal Basilicas of Rome are provided with a sufficient number of Penitentiaries supplied with appropriate faculties.

§ 2. It oversees the proper training of the Penitentiaries appointed in the Papal Basilicas and of those appointed elsewhere.

Art. 193

The Apostolic Penitentiary is charged with the granting and use of indulgences, without prejudice to the competence of the Dicastery for the Doctrine of the Faith concerning their doctrine and of the Dicastery for Divine Worship and the Discipline of the Sacraments for ritual matters.

Supreme Tribunal of the Apostolic Signatura

Art. 194

The Apostolic Signatura functions as the Church's Supreme Tribunal and also ensures that justice in the Church is correctly administered.

Art. 195

§ 1. The Supreme Tribunal of the Apostolic Signatura is composed of Cardinals, Bishops and priests appointed by the Roman Pontiff for a term of five years. It is headed by the Cardinal Prefect.

§ 2. In dispatching the affairs of the Tribunal, the Prefect is assisted by a Secretary.

Art. 196
The Apostolic Signatura, as a tribunal of ordinary jurisdiction, adjudicates:

1. complaints of nullity and petitions for *restitutio in integrum* against sentences of the Roman Rota;

2. recourses in cases involving the status of persons when the Roman Rota has denied a new examination of the case;

3. exceptions of suspicion and other proceedings against judges of the Roman Rota arising from the exercise of their functions;

4. conflicts of competence between tribunals which are not subject to the same appellate tribunal.

Art. 197
§ 1. The Apostolic Signatura, as the administrative tribunal for the Roman Curia, adjudicates recourses against individual administrative acts, whether issued by the Dicasteries or the Secretariat of State or else approved by them, whenever it is contended that the act being impugned violated some law, either in the decision-making process or in the procedure employed.

§ 2. In these cases, in addition to its judgement regarding illegality of the act, the Apostolic Signatura, at the request of the plaintiff, can also judge concerning the reparation of possible damages incurred through the act in question.

§ 3. The Apostolic Signatura also adjudicates other administrative controversies referred to it by the Roman Pontiff or by institutions of the Curia. Finally, it adjudicates conflicts of competence between Dicasteries or between Dicasteries and the Secretariat of State.

Art. 198

The Apostolic Signatura, as an administrative institution of justice in disciplinary matters, is also competent:

1. to exercise vigilance over the correct administration of justice in the different ecclesiastical tribunals and, if need be, to censure officials, advocates or procurators;

2. to adjudicate petitions presented to the Apostolic See for obtaining the referral of a case to the Roman Rota;

3. to adjudicate concerning any other request relative to the administration of justice;

4. to extend the competence of lower tribunals;

5. to grant approval of a tribunal of appeal, as well as approval, if reserved to the Holy See, of the erection of inter-diocesan/inter-eparchial/inter-ritual, regional, national and, if need be, supranational tribunals.

Art. 199

The Apostolic Signatura is governed by its proper law.

Tribunal of the Roman Rota

Art. 200

§ 1. The Tribunal of the Roman Rota ordinarily acts as an appellate court of higher instance at the Apostolic See, with the purpose of safeguarding rights within the Church; it fosters unity of jurisprudence and, by virtue of its decisions, provides assistance to lower tribunals.

§ 2. The Tribunal of the Roman Rota also includes the Office competent to adjudicate the fact of the non-consummation of marriage and the existence of a just cause for granting dispensations.

§ 3. This Office is also competent to deal with cases of the nullity of sacred ordination, pursuant to the norm of universal and proper law, in accordance with the different cases.

Art. 201
§ 1. The Tribunal has a collegiate structure and is composed of a certain number of judges of proven doctrine, competence and experience selected by the Roman Pontiff from various parts of the world.

§ 2. The College of the Tribunal is headed by the Dean, as *primus inter pares*, who is appointed for a term of five years by the Roman Pontiff, who chooses him from among the judges.

§ 3. The Office for procedures of dispensation from a marriage *ratum et non consummatum* and for cases of the nullity of sacred ordination is headed by the Dean, assisted by its proper officials and by designated commissioners and consultors.

Art. 202
§ 1. The Tribunal of the Roman Rota adjudicates in second instance cases that have been decided by ordinary tribunals of first instance and referred to the Holy See by legitimate appeal.

§ 2. It adjudicates in third or further instances cases already decided by the same Apostolic Tribunal and by any other tribunals, unless they have become *res iudicata*.

Art. 203

§ 1. The Roman Rota, in addition, adjudicates in first instance:

1. Bishops in contentious matters, unless they concern the rights or temporal goods of a juridical person represented by the Bishop;

2. Abbots Primate or Abbots Superior of monastic congregations and Supreme Moderators of Institutes of Consecrated Life and Societies of Apostolic Life of Pontifical right;

3. Dioceses/Eparchies or other ecclesiastical persons, whether physical or juridical, which have no Superior below the Roman Pontiff;

4. cases which the Roman Pontiff entrusts to this Tribunal.

§ 2. It adjudicates these same cases also in second and further instances, unless other provisions are made.

Art. 204

The Tribunal of the Roman Rota is governed by its proper law.

VII.
INSTITUTIONS OF FINANCE

Council for the Economy

Art. 205

§ 1. The Council for the Economy is competent for supervising the administrative and financial structures and activities of curial institutions and offices and of institutions associated with the Holy See or that relate to it, as indicated in the list attached to the Council's statutes.

§ 2. The Council for the Economy carries out its functions in the light of the social doctrine of the Church, following the best practices recognized internationally in the field of public administration and striving for an administrative and financial management that is both ethical and efficient.

Art. 206

§ 1. The Council consists of eight Cardinals or Bishops, representing the universality of the Church, and seven lay people, chosen from experts of various nationalities. The fifteen members are appointed by the Roman Pontiff for a five-year term.

§ 2. The Council is convened and chaired by the Cardinal Coordinator, assisted by a Secretary.

§ 3. The Prefect of the Secretariat for the Economy participates in the meetings of the Council, but without the right to vote.

Art. 207

The Council submits for the approval of the Roman Pontiff guidelines and norms aimed at ensuring that:

1. the assets of the entities and administrations subject to its supervision are protected;

2. patrimonial and financial risks are reduced;

3. human, material and financial resources are allocated in a reasonable way and managed with prudence, efficiency and transparency;

4. the agencies and administrations carry out their tasks efficiently, in accordance with the activities, plans and budgets approved in their regard.

Art. 208

The Council establishes the criteria, including that of value, for determining which acts of alienation, acquisition or extraordinary administration carried out by the entities it supervises require, *ad validitatem*, the approval of the Prefect of the Secretariat for the Economy.

Art. 209

§ 1. The Council approves the annual budget and the consolidated financial statements of the Holy See and submits them to the Roman Pontiff.

§ 2. During the vacancy of the Apostolic See, the Council for the Economy provides the Cardinal Camerlengo of the Holy Roman Church with the most recent consolidated financial statements of the Holy See and the budget for the current year.

Art. 210
The Council requests from the Supervisory and Financial Information Authority, whenever necessary and with respect for its operational autonomy, information relevant to the scope of its activities and is informed annually about the activities of the Institute for the Works of Religion.

Art. 211
The Council examines proposals made by the Secretariat for the Economy, as well as eventual suggestions presented by the various administrations of the Holy See, by the Supervisory and Financial Information Authority and by other entities indicated in the Council's proper statutes.

Secretariat for the Economy

Art. 212
§ 1. The Secretariat for the Economy functions as a Papal Secretariat for economic and financial matters.

§ 2. It exercises monitoring and vigilance in administrative, economic and financial matters with regard to curial institutions, offices and other institutions associated with the Holy See or related to it, as indicated in the list attached to the statutes of the Council for the Economy.

§ 3. It also exercises appropriate supervision over Peter's Pence and other papal funds.

Art. 213

§ 1. The Secretariat for the Economy is headed by a Prefect, assisted by a Secretary.

§ 2. The Secretariat has two areas of operation: one for the regulation, monitoring and supervision of economic and financial matters; the other for the regulation, monitoring and supervision of administrative matters.

Art. 214

§ 1. The Secretariat for the Economy must consult the Council for the Economy and submit for its examination proposals and guidelines concerning norms on matters of greater importance or relating to general principles.

§ 2. During the preparation of proposals or guidelines, the Secretariat for the Economy carries out appropriate consultations, with due regard for the autonomy and competencies of the agencies and administrations.

§ 3. For matters relating to relations with states and other subjects of international law, the Secretariat for the Economy acts in cooperation with the Secretariat of State, which has exclusive competence.

Art. 215

The Secretariat for the Economy:

1. issues guidelines on economic and financial matters for the Holy See and verifies that activities are carried out in compliance with the operational plans and approved programmes;

2. monitors the administrative, economic and financial activities of the institutions entrusted to its oversight and supervision and proposes and ensures any corrective actions;

3. prepares the annual budget, verifying that it is respected, and the consolidated balance sheet of the Holy See, and submits these to the Council for the Economy;

4. carries out an annual risk assessment of the patrimonial and financial situation of the Holy See and submits it to the Council for the Economy.

Art. 216
The Secretariat for the Economy:

1. formulates guidelines, policies, models and procedures with regard to procurement, aimed at ensuring that all the goods and services needed by curial institutions and by offices and institutions associated with the Holy See or related to it, are acquired in the most prudent, efficient and economically advantageous manner, in conformity with appropriate internal audits and procedures;

2. arranges for suitable information technology so that administrative, economic and financial management will be effective and transparent and that archives and accounting records are faithfully kept, in accordance with approved norms and procedures.

Art. 217
§ 1. The Secretariat for the Economy includes the Human Resources Department of the Holy See, which, in dialogue and cooperation with the entities concerned, is responsible for whatever concerns the position and labour management of the personnel of entities subject to the Holy See's proper legislation, without prejudice to the provisions of art. 48, 2°.

§ 2. Among its other areas of competence, the Secretariat for the Economy, through this Department, authorizes the hiring of personnel, verifying that all necessary requisites have been met, and approves the organizational charts of the entities.

Art. 218

§ 1. The Secretariat for the Economy approves, based on the criteria determined by the Council for the Economy, all acts of alienation, acquisition or extraordinary administration carried out by curial institutions and offices and institutions associated with the Holy See or related to it, for which the Secretariat's approval is required *ad validitatem.*

§ 2. During the vacancy of the Apostolic See, the Secretariat for the Economy furnishes the Cardinal Camerlengo of the Holy Roman Church whatever information may be requested with regard to the financial status of the Holy See.

Administration of the Patrimony of the Apostolic See

Art. 219

§ 1. The Administration of the Patrimony of the Apostolic See is the entity responsible for the administration and management of the real estate and movable assets of the Holy See which are meant to provide the resources necessary for the Roman Curia properly to carry out its work for the good of, and in service to, the particular Churches.

§ 2. It is also responsible for administering the real estate and movable assets of those entities that have entrusted their assets to the Holy See, respecting the specific purpose for which those assets were established and the guidelines and general policies approved by the competent institutions.

§ 3. The execution of the financial transactions referred to in §§ 1 and 2 is carried out through the Institute for the Works of Religion.

Art. 220

§ 1. The Administration of the Patrimony of the Apostolic See provides whatever is necessary for the ordinary activities of the Roman Curia, and is responsible for liquidity, accounting, purchases and other services.

§ 2. The Administration of the Patrimony of the Apostolic See can provide the same services referred to in § 1 also for institutions associated with the Holy See or related to it, in the event that they request it, or if so stipulated.

Art. 221

§ 1. The Administration of the Patrimony of the Apostolic See is headed by a President, assisted by a Secretary and a council made up of Cardinals, Bishops, priests and lay people, which helps him in developing the strategic guidelines of the Administration and evaluating its outcomes.

§ 2. The internal organization of the Administration has three functional areas, responsible for property management, financial affairs and services.

§ 3. The Adminstration makes use of the advice of experts in the areas of its competence, appointed pursuant to Articles 16-17 § 1.

Office of the Auditor General

Art. 222

The Auditor General's Office is charged with auditing the consolidated financial statements of the Holy See.

Art. 223

§ 1. In accordance with the annual audit plan approved by the Council for the Economy, the Office is responsible for auditing the annual financial statements of individual curial institutions and offices, and those of institutions associated with the Holy See or related to it, that are included in the aforementioned consolidated financial statements.

§ 2. The annual audit plan is submitted by the Auditor General to the Council for the Economy for its approval.

Art. 224

§ 1. The Office of the Auditor General, at the request of the Council for the Economy, or the Secretariat for the Economy, or the heads of the offices and administrations referred to in art. 205 § 1, carries out audits in particular situations connected to: anomalies in the use or allocation of financial or material resources; irregularities in the granting of contracts or in the execution of transactions or alienations; acts of corruption or fraud. These audits can be initiated independently by the Auditor General, who informs the Cardinal Coordinator of the Council for the Economy beforehand, citing the reasons.

§ 2. The Auditor General receives notifications from individuals who in the course of their work become aware of particular situations. After studying these notifications, he presents them with a report to the Prefect of the Secretariat for the Economy and also, should he deem it necessary, to the Cardinal Coordinator of the Council for the Economy.

Commission for Confidential Matters

Art. 225

The Commission for Confidential Matters is competent:

1. to authorize any legal, economic or financial act that for the greater good of the Church or of persons must be kept confidential and removed from the examination and supervision of the competent entities;

2. to monitor contracts of the Holy See which by law demand confidentiality and to exercise vigilance over them.

Art. 226
The Commission, in accordance with its proper statutes, is composed of members appointed by the Roman Pontiff for a term of five years. It is headed by a President, assisted by a Secretary.

Committee for Investments

Art. 227
§ 1. The Committee for Investments is responsible for guaranteeing the ethical nature of the Holy See's equity investments in accordance with the Church's social doctrine and, at the same time, ensuring their profitability, propriety and degree of risk.

§ 2. In accordance with its statutes, the Committee is composed of members and distinguished professionals appointed for a term of five years by the Roman Pontiff. It is headed by a President, assisted by a Secretary.

VIII.
OFFICES

Prefecture of the Papal Household

Art. 228

§ 1. The Prefecture is responsible for the internal organization of the Papal Household and supervises whatever concerns the conduct and service of all who make up the Papal Chapel and the Papal Family.

§ 2. It is headed by a Prefect, assisted by the Regent, both appointed by the Roman Pontiff for a term of five years, assisted by several officials.

Art. 229

§ 1. The Prefecture of the Papal Household sees to the planning and execution, apart from their strictly liturgical aspect, of papal ceremonies and determines the order of precedence.

§ 2. It is the task of the Prefecture to coordinate the services of the antechamber and to organize the public, special and private audiences of the Roman Pontiff and the visits of individual persons, in consultation with the Secretariat of State whenever circumstances so demand. It makes all the necessary arrangements when Heads of State, Heads of Government, government ministers, public authorities and other dignitaries, as well as ambassadors, are received by the Pontiff in solemn audience.

§ 3. It is also responsible for arranging the spiritual exercises of the Roman Pontiff, the College of Cardinals and the Roman Curia.

Art. 230

§ 1. The Prefecture is responsible for making preparations whenever the Roman Pontiff visits the territory of the Vatican or Rome, or travels within Italy.

§ 2. The Prefect assists the Pope only on the occasion of meetings and visits that take place within Vatican territory.

Office for the Liturgical Celebrations of the Supreme Pontiff

Art. 231

§ 1. The Office for the Liturgical Celebrations of the Supreme Pontiff is responsible for preparing whatever is needed for the liturgical and other sacred celebrations in the Vatican at which the Roman Pontiff, or – in his name and by his mandate – a Cardinal or a Prelate presides, participates or assists, and for supervising them according to the current prescriptions of liturgical law. It also arranges everything necessary or useful for their dignified celebration and for the active participation of the faithful.

§ 2. The Office is also responsible for the preparation and execution of all papal liturgical celebrations that take place during the pastoral visits of the Roman Pontiff and his Apostolic Journeys, bearing in mind the distinctive characteristics of papal celebrations.

Art. 232

§ 1. The Office is headed by the Master of Papal Liturgical Celebrations, appointed by the Roman Pontiff for a term of five years. He is assisted in sacred celebrations by the Papal Masters of Ceremony, appointed by the Roman Pontiff for five years.

§ 2. Within the Office, the Master is assisted by various officials and consultors.

Art. 233

§ 1. The Master of Papal Liturgical Celebrations is also responsible for the papal sacristy and for the chapels of the Apostolic Palace.

§ 2. He is likewise responsible for the Sistine Chapel Choir, with the duty of overseeing all the Choir's liturgical, pastoral, spiritual, artistic and educational areas and activities. The Sistine Chapel Choir has been joined to the Office because it offers a specific service to papal liturgical functions and in order to preserve and promote the prestigious artistic and musical heritage produced over the centuries by the Choir itself for the solemn liturgies of the Pontiffs.

Art. 234

The competence of the Office includes the celebration of the Consistory and the direction of the liturgical celebrations of the College of Cardinals during the vacancy of the Apostolic See.

The Camerlengo of the Holy Roman Church

Art. 235

§ 1. The Cardinal Camerlengo of the Holy Roman Church carries out the duties assigned to him by the special law governing the vacancy of the Apostolic See and the election of the Roman Pontiff.

§ 2. The Cardinal Camerlengo of the Holy Roman Church and the Vice-Camerlengo are appointed by the Roman Pontiff.

§ 3. In carrying out his assigned duties, the Cardinal Camerlengo of the Holy Roman Church is helped by three Cardinal Assistants under his authority and responsibility. One of these is the Cardinal Coordinator of the Council for the Economy and the other two are selected in accordance with the modalities set forth in the norms concerning the vacancy of the Apostolic See and the election of the Roman Pontiff.

Art. 236

The task of overseeing and administering the temporal goods and rights of the Apostolic See during the time of its vacancy is entrusted to the Cardinal Camerlengo of the Holy Roman Church. If he is impeded, this function will be assumed by the Vice-Camerlengo.

Art. 237

During the vacancy of the Apostolic See, it is the right and duty of the Cardinal Camerlengo of the Holy Roman Church:

1. to request from all administrations dependent on the Holy See reports on their patrimonial and economic status, as well as information on any extraordinary business that may be under way;

2. to request from the Council for the Economy the budget and consolidated financial statement of the Holy See for the previous year, as well as the budget for the following year;

3. to request, to the extent necessary, from the Secretariat for the Economy any information on the financial status of the Holy See.

IX.
ADVOCATES

Register of Advocates at the Roman Curia

Art. 238

In addition to the Register of Advocates of the Roman Rota, a Register is kept of Advocates who, at the request of interested parties, are authorized to represent them in their cases before the Supreme Tribunal of the Apostolic Signatura and offer their assistance in hierarchical recourses lodged before curial institutions.

Art. 239

§ 1. Professionals distinguished by virtue of their suitable preparation as evidenced by academic degrees, their exemplary Christian life, and their honourable character and professional ability, can be inscribed in this Register.

§ 2. The Secretary of State, after hearing a Commission stably constituted for this purpose, provides for inscribing in the Register those experts in possession of the requisites referred to in § 1 who so request it. In the event that those requisites cease, the Advocates are removed from the Register.

The Corps of Advocates of the Holy See

Art. 240

§ 1. The Corps of Advocates of the Holy See is preferably composed of those inscribed in the Register of Advocates at the Roman Curia. They can undertake the representation of cases before ecclesiastical or civil tribunals in the name of the Holy See or of curial institutions.

§ 2. The Advocates of the Holy See are appointed by the Secretary of State for a five-year period, renewable, after hearing the Commission referred to in Art. 239 § 2; they cease from office upon completion of their seventy-fifth year of age, and they can be dismissed for serious reasons.

§ 3. The Advocates of the Holy See are obliged to lead an upright and exemplary Christian life and to carry out the tasks entrusted to them with the utmost conscientiousness and for the good of the Church.

X.
INSTITUTIONS ASSOCIATED
WITH THE HOLY SEE

Art. 241

There are certain institutions, either of ancient origin or more recent establishment, that, albeit not part of the Roman Curia in the strict sense and having their own juridical personality, nevertheless provide a variety of useful or necessary services to the Roman Pontiff, the Roman Curia and the universal Church, and are in some way associated with the Curia itself.

Art. 242

The Vatican Apostolic Archive carries out its specific activity of preserving and maintaining acts and documents concerning the government of the universal Church, so that they can be available primarily to the Holy See and the Roman Curia in the fulfilment of their activities, and, secondarily, by papal concession, so that they can represent for all scholars, without distinction of country or religion, sources for the knowledge, including secular knowledge, of events that in the course of history have been closely connected with the life of the Church.

Art. 243

An institution of ancient origin, the Vatican Apostolic Library is an outstanding means for the Church to contribute to the development and dissemination of culture, in support of the work of the Apostolic See. Through its various sections, it is responsible for collecting and preserving a vast patrimony of learning and art and of making it available to scholars in search of truth.

Art. 244

The Fabric of Saint Peter's deals with everything that concerns the Papal Basilica of Saint Peter, which preserves the memory of the martyrdom and the tomb of the Apostle, including the conservation and decorum of the building and the internal discipline of its employees and of pilgrims and visitors, in accordance with its proper norms. Where necessary, the President and the Secretary of the Fabric act in agreement with the Chapter of the Basilica.

Art. 245

The Pontifical Commission for Sacred Archaeology is responsible for studying, preserving, safeguarding and enhancing the Christian catacombs of Italy, in which the testimonies of faith and art of the first Christian communities continue to transmit their profound message to pilgrims and visitors.

Art. 246

For the pursuit of truth and its dissemination in the various areas of the divine and human sciences, there have arisen within the Catholic Church different Academies, among which the Pontifical Academy of Sciences, the Pontifical Academy of Social Sciences and the Pontifical Academy for Life stand out.

Art. 247

In order to promote and develop a culture of quality within academic institutions directly dependent on the Holy See and to ensure their quality standards are valid at the international level, the Holy See has established the Agency for the Evaluation and Promotion of Quality in Ecclesiastical Universities and Faculties.

Art. 248

The Supervisory and Financial Information Authority carries out, as provided for by law and by its proper statutes, the functions of: supervision aimed at the prevention and countering of money laundering and the financing of terrorism with regard to the entities and subjects under its supervision; prudential supervision of those entities that carry out a financial activity on a professional basis; regulation for prudential purposes of those entities that carry out a financial activity on a professional basis and, in the cases provided for by law, regulation for the prevention and countering of money laundering and financing of terrorism. In this capacity, it also carries out the function of financial intelligence.

Art. 249

With regard to their constitution and administration, all the aforementioned institutions associated with the Holy See are governed by their proper laws.

XI.
TRANSITIONAL NORM

Art. 250

§ 1. The general provisions of the norms of this Apostolic Constitution apply to the Secretariat of State and to the Dicasteries, Institutions, Offices, and institutions that are part of the Roman Curia or are associated with the Holy See. Those that also have proper statutes and laws are to observe them only insofar as they do not conflict with the present Apostolic Constitution, and are to submit their planned adaptation as soon as possible for the approval of the Roman Pontiff.

§ 2. The executory norms currently in force for the entities mentioned in § 1, such as the "General Regulations of the Roman Curia", the *Ordo servandus* and the internal *modus procedendi* of curial institutions and offices, are to be observed in everything that is not contrary to the norms of this Apostolic Constitution, until the approval of the new *Ordo servandus* and statutes.

§ 3. With the entry into force of this Apostolic Constitution, the Constitution *Pastor Bonus* is completely abrogated and replaced; with it, the institutions of the Roman Curia indicated in *Pastor Bonus* and no longer provided for or reorganized in this Constitution are also abolished.

I decree the present Apostolic Constitution to be firm, valid and effective, now and henceforth, entering into full effect beginning on 5 June 2022, the Solemnity of Pentecost, and that it be fully observed in all its details by those to whom it applies, now and in the future, anything to the contrary notwithstanding, even if worthy of most special mention.

Given in Rome, at Saint Peter's, on the Solemnity of Saint Joseph, Spouse of the Blessed Virgin Mary, on 19 March in the year 2022, the tenth of my Pontificate.

Francis

NOTES

1. JOHN PAUL II, Encyclical Letter *Redemptoris Missio*, 2.

2. FRANCIS, Apostolic Exhortation *Evangelii Gaudium*, 24.

3. Cf. ibid., 30.

4. FRANCIS, Encyclical Letter *Lumen Fidei*, 4.

5. Cf. SECOND VATICAN ECUMENICAL COUNCIL, Decree *Christus Dominus*, 9ff.

6. JOHN PAUL II, Apostolic Exhortation *Christifideles Laici*, 32.

7. FRANCIS, *Address for the Commemoration of the Fiftieth Anniversary of the Establishment of the Synod of Bishops* (17 October 2015).

8. Ibid.

9. Cf. SECOND VATICAN ECUMENICAL COUNCIL, Dogmatic Constitution *Lumen Gentium*, 19.

10. Cf. ibid., 20.

11. Cf. ibid., 8.

12. Cf. ibid., 22; cf. JOHN PAUL II, Apostolic Exhortation *Pastores Gregis*, 8, 55, 56.

13. *Ibidem*, 23.

14. Cf. SECOND VATICAN ECUMENICAL COUNCIL, Dogmatic Constitution *Lumen Gentium,* 18; FIRST VATICAN ECUMENICAL COUNCIL, Dogmatic Constitution *Pastor Aeternus*, Preamble.

15. Cf. ibid., 23.

16. Cf. JOHN PAUL II, Apostolic Exhortation *Pastores Gregis*, 63.

17. Cf. ibid.

18. Cf. JOHN PAUL II, Apostolic Letter Motu Proprio *Apostolos Suos*, 12.

19. SECOND VATICAN ECUMENICAL COUNCIL, Dogmatic Constitution *Lumen Gentium*, 30.

20. FRANCIS, Apostolic Exhortation *Evangelii Gaudium*, 120.

21. Cf. SECOND VATICAN ECUMENICAL COUNCIL, Dogmatic Constitution *Lumen Gentium*, 30.

22. PAUL VI, *Address at the Final Public Session of the Second Vatican Ecumenical Council* (7 December 1965).

23. FRANCIS, *Greeting to the Cardinals Gathered for the Consistory* (12 February 2015).

24. SECOND VATICAN ECUMENICAL COUNCIL, Decree *Christus Dominus*, 9.

25. SECOND VATICAN ECUMENICAL COUNCIL, Dogmatic Constitution *Lumen Gentium*, 18.

26. Ibid., 23.

27. Cf. FRANCIS, Apostolic Exhortation *Evangelii Gaudium*, 16.

28. Cf. SECOND VATICAN ECUMENICAL COUNCIL, Dogmatic Constitution *Dei Verbum*, 7.

29. Cf. FRANCIS, Apostolic Exhortation *Evangelii Gaudium*, 31-32.

30. Cf. SECOND VATICAN ECUMENICAL COUNCIL, Dogmatic Constitution *Lumen Gentium*, 8.

31. PAUL VI, *Homily for the Solemnity of the Immaculate Conception of the Blessed Virgin Mary* at the conclusion of the Second Vatican Ecumenical Council (8 December 1965).